The Complete Book of the
Dinosaur

The Complete Book of the Dinosaur

Joseph Wallace

GALLERY BOOKS
An Imprint of W. H. Smith Publishers, Inc.
112 Madison Avenue
New York, New York 10016

A FRIEDMAN GROUP BOOK

Published by Gallery Books
An imprint of W. H. Smith Publishers, Inc.
112 Madison Avenue
New York, New York 10016

ISBN 0-8317-2362-9

THE COMPLETE BOOK OF THE DINOSAUR
was prepared and produced by
Michael Friedman Publishing Group, Inc.
15 West 26th Street
New York, NY 10010

Editor: Sharon Kalman
Art Director: Robert W. Kosturko
Designer: David B. Weisman
Photography Editor: Christopher C. Bain
Production Manager: Karen L. Greenberg

Macintosh output by Line & Tone Typografix Corp.
Color separations by Universal Colour Scanning Ltd.
Printed and bound in Italy
by Grafiche Alma - Milano

Dedication: For my most careful readers, all of whom are less than four feet tall.

The Complete Book Of The

saur

A visitor to the age of the dinosaurs would encounter an eerie, unfamiliar landscape filled with a mixture of strange and recognizable animals.

Introduction:
The Dinosaurs' Day

© Doug Henderson

Daybreak Welcome to the dawn of the dinosaurs.

Like countless mornings before it, this one is humid and hazy. The sun climbs above a rugged, hilly horizon, and looks down on a vast expanse of land swathed in heavy mist. The day is already uncomfortably warm; by midday it will be hot, as it always gets hot in this ancient tropical world.

The mist begins to rise, giving you your first glimpse of an eerie, alien landscape. A few things are immediately obvious: There are no trees growing here, no mighty oaks or spreading chestnuts. Scanning the fertile earth around you, you note that such familiar plants as tulips and azaleas are absent—in fact, there are no flowers of any sort. And there's something else missing, something you take for granted in your temperate twentieth-century world. That's right—grass! Where's the grass?

Now you recall learning that trees, flowering plants, and grasses wouldn't appear for millions of years. You'll report that although scientists were right about that, the world of the first dinosaurs is far from barren. Ferns of many different types grow in abundance, some stretching above your head toward the sky. Around a nearby lake (populated by salamanders that look surprisingly similar to the ones you know from back home), you see other plants, tall, spiky ones that your guidebook identifies as horsetails.

So where are the dinosaurs? Besides the salamanders and a creature that surfaced briefly in the middle of the lake—possibly an alligator or crocodile—you've seen nothing.

Maybe there aren't any dinosaurs here. Your course was set for 230 million years ago: Maybe you were sent back too far. But wait—something is rustling in the ferns on the lake's opposite shore. Unaware of your presence, it moves ponderously into view. Yes, it's a big reptile, with a massive, toothy head and thick legs, but it doesn't look like any of the dinosaurs in your book. Instead, it resembles a crocodile with a glandular condition. It's a thecodont, one of the dinosaur's direct ancestors.

That's better—but it's still not a dinosaur. You're running out of time, so you'd better head back to your ship. Hope it works. You'd hate to be stuck here forever.

Midmorning

You have traveled forward several million years (it's now about 195 million years ago), but the landscape hasn't changed all that much. The ferns and horsetails do look a little different, but you still don't see any grasses or flowering plants. There have been a few developments: Distant hillsides harbor dark groves of pine trees, and that nearby gingko tree looks just like the one growing outside your apartment building.

But you can't spend too much time looking at the plants, because you are here to hunt for dinosaurs. At first your luck is no better than it was a few million years ago: You see nothing but frogs, a tortoise, and some enormous dragonflies. It's interesting enough, but nothing to write home about—if you could write home.

Then something rustles in the ferns near your feet. You jump, it jumps, and you get a quick glimpse of a tiny, shrewlike creature. It gives you a horrified glance, then scuttles away.

A mammal, for heaven's sake. You didn't come all this way to spot a mammal. They have plenty of those at home, and all of them are more impressive than this scrawny, ancient rat.

Fortunately, your streak of bad luck soon changes,

The world of the Triassic was a swampy, humid one, inhabited by ancient reptiles that most closely resembled modern alligators and crocodiles.

and you finally see your first dinosaur. It's nowhere near as impressive as some you've read about, but it's definitely a dinosaur, a svelte 10-foot (3-meter) reptile speeding across a nearby valley on two powerful legs. Your guidebook tells you that this is *Coelophysis*, and though you know it eats only small animals, its long, toothy jaw looks quite capable of dismembering a human. So you're not unhappy when it heads off and disappears from view.

That seems to be all, at least in this area. Your heart still pounding from your recent glimpse of an actual dinosaur, you climb back into your ship and set your sights ahead about fifty million years. You know you should see some big changes.

Afternoon

You wanted changes? You got them. In the millions of years since you last touched down, the world seems to have gotten wetter. A huge inland sea laps gently against a muddy shore, stagnant marshes stretch for miles, and lazy rivers wind through groves of ferns, palmlike cycads, and other plants. Towering pines blanket higher ground, forming dark groves hiding who-knows-what terrifying creatures.

From your hillside perch, you immediately see that dinosaurs and other creatures are much more common now than they were in your previous stops. Down below, a herd of 80-foot (24-meter) *Diplodocus* rumble through

In the Late Triassic, the visitor would finally begin to spot some familiar dinosaurs, like these wary, fleet-footed *Coelophysis*.

the mud on legs like cathedral columns, their long necks and tails swaying as they walk. A hundred yards away, their mouths open to reveal shining, knifelike teeth, a pair of huge *Allosaurs* stalk the edge of a pine grove. Seemingly unafraid, a *Stegosaurus*, its row of leathery plates absorbing the warm sunlight, crops some tender vegetation from the lower branches of a tall tree. Out in the marsh, a bizarre creature lifts its snakelike head from the water, while above a pterosaur glides on leathery wings that resemble great skin sails.

Gazing at this lively scene, you wonder how the world ever changed so much that the dinosaurs, pterosaurs, and other giant reptiles disappeared. But you know that the world did change, and all of these creatures and their descendants became extinct roughly sixty-five million years before you embarked on your journey through time. How did it happen? Finding out was the main goal of your risky trip. So now you'd better set your compass for the very end of the dinosaurs' reign.

Dusk

At first glance, you think you must have gone off course. This can't be the dinosaurs' last gasp—they look too abundant and healthy. On the plains below, you see vast herds of three-horned *Triceratops* stampeding along like buffalo. Further away a single *Tyrannosaurus* strides toward an unknown destination. With its huge jaws and 7-inch (18-centimeter) teeth, it is a spectacularly powerful predator.

That's not all. A colony of odd duck-billed dinosaurs, 30 feet (9 meters) long and boasting outlandish crests, browses at the edge of a grove of trees. Nearby, a small, unidentifiable dinosaur (could this be a species unknown to modern scientists?) races along on two legs, as if pursued by ghosts. And a stolid *Ankylosaurus* trudges past, dragging its clubbed tail like deadweight.

So what did bring an end to this vibrant scene? You note a few hints. There's a new chill in the air, almost a taste of fall after a nearly endless summertime. On the

Following Page: © Doug Henderson

horizon, three active volcanoes belch black soot into the air, where it is caught by the wind and carried high into the atmosphere.

Even as you stand gazing at the volcanoes, the ground shifts under your feet. This earthquake is strong enough to send the *Triceratops* herd thundering across the plain. You and your ship are fine, but a distant hill seems to split asunder, and a stream of hot lava glows red as it pours toward the valley.

Were the change in the climate, the volcanoes, and the earthquakes responsible for the death of the dinosaurs? Or was there, as some modern scientists believe, an outside cause, a gigantic comet or asteroid that crashed to earth, dooming the great reptiles? There's no way to tell, and it's too dangerous to stick around to see. You won't do any good if you die out with the *Tyrannosaurs*, *Triceratops*, and others.

It's time to head home and fill in the details of what you just witnessed: the 160-million-year reign of some of the most widespread, adaptable, and varied animals ever to live on earth.

If scientists do invent a time machine someday, the world of the dinosaurs will be high on the list of the most popular places to go. And if experts *were* able to travel back to that ancient era, their observations would certainly answer many of the most fascinating questions we still ask of the great reptiles: Were they warm-blooded? Did they care for their young like mammals, or abandon their eggs, as most modern reptiles do? How did they hunt? And, of course, what caused them to die?

Yet even without time travel, scientists have been able to develop convincing theories about these and many other dinosaur puzzles. With the help of fossils and other relics of that distant age, researchers have been able to paint a vivid, remarkably detailed portrait of the dinosaurs, the creatures that lived before, with, and after them, and—of course—the fascinating world they inhabited.

Previous page: Watch out for stampeding sauropods! Throughout the age of the dinosaurs, environmental cataclysms killed vast numbers of the great reptiles—and left fossils for us to discover millions of years later.

Right: Dinosaurs may never have been more abundant than in Late Cretaceous North America, where *Tyrannosaurus* and *Triceratops* were just two of the many familiar species.

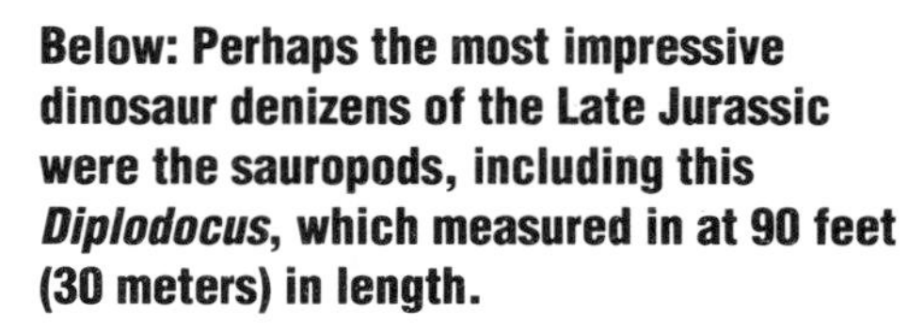

Below: Perhaps the most impressive dinosaur denizens of the Late Jurassic were the sauropods, including this *Diplodocus*, which measured in at 90 feet (30 meters) in length.

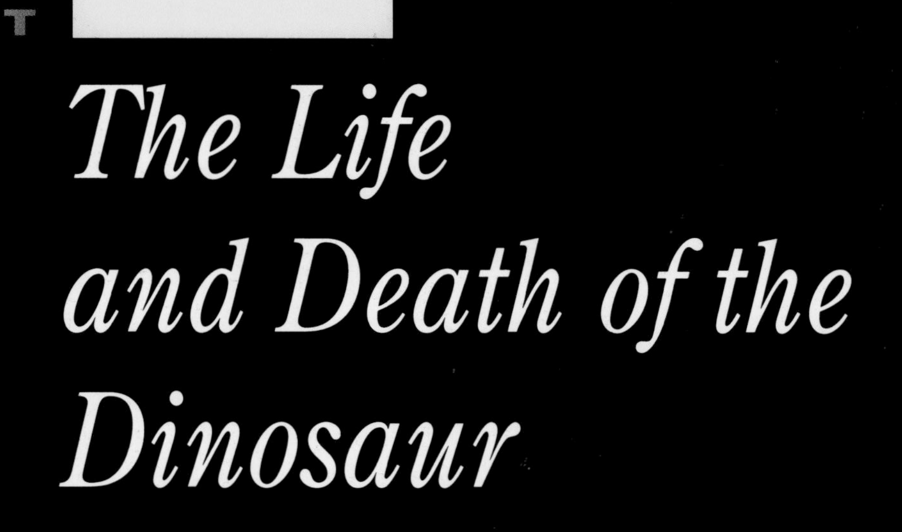

P A R T 1

The Life and Death of the Dinosaur

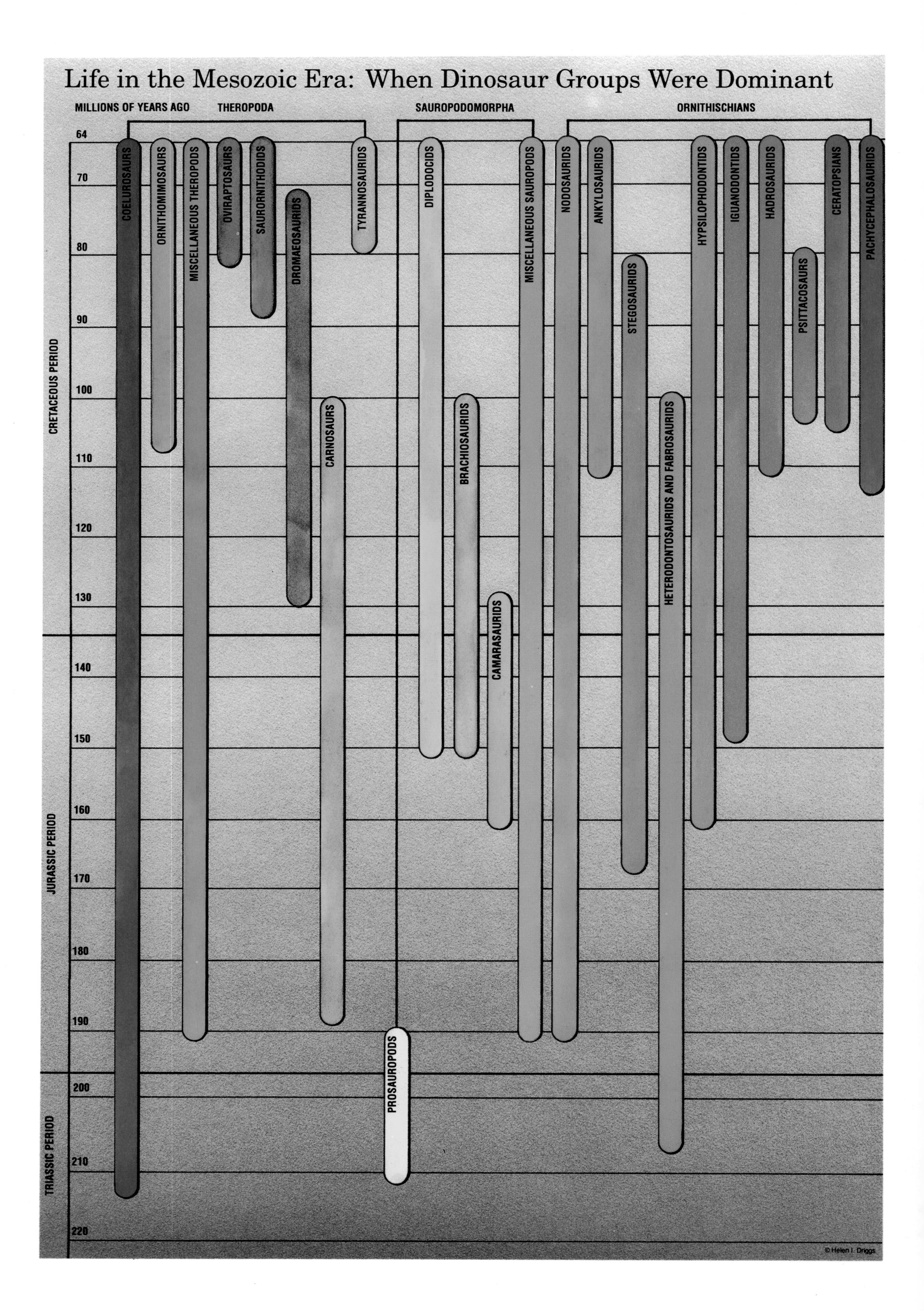

Life in the Mesozoic Era: When Dinosaur Groups Were Dominant
MILLIONS OF YEARS AGO
THEROPODA
SAUROPODOMORPHA
ORNITHISCHIANS
64
70
80
90
100
110
120
130
140
150
160
170
180
190
200
210
220
CRETACEOUS PERIOD
JURASSIC PERIOD
TRIASSIC PERIOD
COELUROSAURS
ORNITHOMIMOSAURS
MISCELLANEOUS THEROPODS
OVIRAPTOSAURS
SAURORNITHODIDS
DROMAEOSAURIDS
TYRANNOSAURIDS
CARNOSAURS
DIPLODOCIDS
BRACHIOSAURIDS
CAMARASAURIDS
MISCELLANEOUS SAUROPODS
PROSAUROPODS
NODOSAURIDS
ANKYLOSAURIDS
STEGOSAURIDS
HETERODONTOSAURIDS AND FABROSAURIDS
HYPSILOPHODONTIDS
IGUANODONTIDS
HADROSAURIDS
PSITTACOSAURS
CERATOPSIANS
PACHYCEPHALOSAURIDS
© Helen I. Driggs

These Came First

The dinosaur family tree is a complex, ever-changing map of our knowledge of the great reptiles. Most scientists believe it is accurate, if incomplete; others think a major reorganization is due.

Quick, name something that lived before the dinosaurs.

Can't do it? Don't be embarrassed; you're in good company. A remarkable number of people know a great deal about the dinosaurs—how they lived, what their sex lives were like, why they died—but draw a blank when it comes to putting the great reptiles in the context of the history of life on earth. Sure, we all learned something about the primordial soup in school, and we can guess that simple microorganisms and plants may have predated the dinosaurs. But that's about it.

Most people are amazed to learn that the dinosaurs were actually very late arrivals on the planet. After all, they didn't show up until about 225 million years ago, during the Triassic period. By contrast, scientists now believe that the earth itself is about 4.5 billion years old, and that the first life appeared about a billion years later, roughly 3.5 billion years ago.

Below: Volcanoes and other great forces helped build the earth, paving the way for plants and, eventually, increasing animal life.

Of course, we're not talking about advanced forms of life here. The first creatures on earth were, indeed, one-celled organisms similar to today's bacteria. In fact, none of the life that evolved during the Precambrian eon (which lasted from the dawn of the earth through about 600 million years ago) was very complex. Bacteria and simple blue-green algae were about it for more than two billion years.

The arrival of blue-green algae may have been the most important development in the history of the earth. These simple plants were the first to practice photosynthesis, and, as we all learned in school, a by-product of photosynthesis is oxygen. The oxygen created by ancient algae opened the door for more advanced air-breathing animals to develop.

Even then, the multi-celled creatures that spread through the oceans a billion years ago were simple worms and plants. Not until another 300 million years passed did more complex animals appear: jellyfish, early corals, sponges, and others. We learned of them from fossils found in Australia, Canada, and elsewhere.

The pace finally began to pick up about 550 to 600 million years ago, at the onset of the Paleozoic era ("the era of ancient life"), which lasted almost until the dawn of the dinosaurs. The first subdivision of the Paleozoic era was the Cambrian period, which lasted about seventy million years. During this time, more advanced jellyfish, worms, and mollusks appeared, as did fishlike creatures and trilobites—those odd, segmented creatures whose remains are so abundant that they can be found in any store that sells fossils.

The first primitive plants to colonize the land didn't appear until the end of the Ordovician period (500 to 430 million years ago). Far more abundant were mollusks and bizarre, primitive jawless fishes that resembled today's lampreys.

The Silurian period (430 to 395 million years ago) saw the arrival of the first jawed fishes, but it was the Devonian (395 to 345 million years ago) that hosted an explosion in the number and diversity of these fishes. Early sharks swam the seas and lakes, and other fish began to take on more amphibious characteristics. Meanwhile, millipedes and centipedes began to colonize the land, as did tree ferns and other plants. The pace of evolution was clearly quickening.

The Mississipian and Pennsylvanian periods (known together in Europe as the Carboniferous period), lasting from 345 to 280 million years ago, saw that quickened pace continue. By the end of these two periods, humid forests covered most of the land, and the seas and lakes were filled with fish and other creatures. On land, gigantic dragonflies, centipedes, spiders, and a host of insects haunted the swamps. Amphibians, including some of the largest ever, flourished.

One of the most ancient of all insects, the dragonfly has survived with little change for hundreds of millions of years. Early individuals, like this monster, had wingspans of 2 feet (60 centimeters) or more.

Many-segmented trilobites (top) were among the most abundant of all sea animals during the Ordovician, but disappeared in a mass extinction rivaling the one that ended the reign of the dinosaurs.

But perhaps the most important development of the Late Carboniferous was the appearance of the first reptiles, which evolved from amphibians into creatures completely suited to dry land. With their leathery, watertight eggs, the reptiles could venture much further inland than the amphibians, who were forced to lay their soft eggs in water.

These first reptiles, such as the cotylosaurs, were just one step on a road that would eventually lead to the dinosaurs. But you wouldn't know it to look at them, as they were small, nondescript insect-eaters.

Next came the Permian period (280 to 245 million years ago), the last period in the Paleozoic era and the last before the rise of the dinosaurs. New types of plants and animals were abundant everywhere, including many that closely resembled those we see today. Gingko trees and the first conifers spread across drier areas, often forming dense forests. Insects were everywhere, although few reached the great sizes seen earlier (the dragonfly with a 2-foot [60-centimeter] wingspan was disappearing). Large amphibians colonized swampy areas in great numbers.

But the most dramatic development in the Permian was the rise of the large reptiles—including the synapsids, which evolved, remarkably, into all mammals. The earliest synapsids (also known as mammal-like reptiles) were the pelycosaurs, plodding beasts that wore great sails of skin and bone across their backs. Perhaps the best known of all pelycosaurs was *Dimetrodon*; like the others, it probably used its sail to vent excess heat on warm days, and to gather rays from the sun when the temperature was cool.

Later in the Permian, a new type of synapsid evolved from the pelycosaurs. The therapsids, the most advanced branch of synapsids, are among the most fascinating of all early animals. They were clearly the most advanced animals of their time, and many of their features (including greater agility, a more advanced respiratory system, and teeth better adapted to meat-eating) closely resembled those of mammals, not reptiles. For millions of years, the therapsids were the dominant animals on earth.

But their empire was not to last through the Triassic period (245 to 193 million years ago), the first in the Mesozoic era ("the era of middle life"). In the Triassic, new types of reptiles began to emerge. These were the archosaurs, or "ruling reptiles," whose earliest representatives were the thecodonts.

© Doug Henderson

Hidden among the trees and watercourses of this peaceful Triassic scene were early mammals, giant insects, huge salamanders, and perhaps the first dinosaurs.

At first, the thecodonts didn't seem to be much of a threat to the therapsids. After all, the early thecodonts were sluggish, sprawling creatures that most closely resembled crocodiles. But a gradual development took place among the thecodonts during their millions of years on earth, an evolution that enabled them to adapt and win the long struggle for survival from the mammal-like reptiles.

The most important change in the thecodonts was skeletal. All previous reptiles were "sprawlers," meaning that their legs swung out from the sides of their bodies, leaving their bellies resting on the ground. This posture gave the reptiles a powerful, steady stride, but not a fast or agile one.

As the Triassic progressed, the thecodonts' bone structure gradually changed: Their legs moved under the body, giving them a far more erect stance than any previous reptile. At the same time, their hind legs lengthened and developed powerful muscles. With this advanced posture, such thecodonts as the *Euparkia* and the later *Ornithosuchus* could rear up on their hind legs, balance with their stiff tails, and move with surprising speed. More primitive reptiles simply couldn't compete.

But, despite these evolutionary advantages, the thecodonts' reign was a short—though extremely influential—one. They would not survive the Triassic, but their descendants would last far longer. In fact, two groups, the crocodilians and the birds, still thrive today. Another, the pterosaurs, lasted for more than a hundred million years.

But a fourth group that descended from the thecodonts was by far the most impressive of all. It contained, as you've probably guessed, some of the most famous animals ever found on earth: the dinosaurs. For the next 160 million years, they populated every corner of the globe. And even today, sixty-five million years after the last one died, their story is still being written.

The magnificent mammal-like reptile *Dimetrodon*, a common resident of the Early Permian, boasted a great sail of skin and bone along its back.

Classification:
Putting Dinosaurs In Their Place

That doesn't give you a very secure feeling about the accuracy of the upcoming section, does it? Well, think of how the poor paleontologists feel; they're the ones who've been trying for nearly a century and a half to "classify" dinosaurs, to figure out exactly where the great extinct reptiles fit into the grand scheme of all life on earth.

It's not an easy job, and—despite powerful new technology and an abundance of brilliant scientific minds addressing the problem—completely accurate classification looks as if it may always remain a dream.

Although people undoubtedly have been finding dinosaur bones throughout history, 1822 saw the unearthing of the first bone ever recognized as having belonged to a gigantic extinct reptile (see page 173 for details). But the true discovery of the dinosaurs didn't occur for another seventeen years. And even then, it took a remarkable imaginative leap by paleontologist Richard Owen to put dinosaurs on the map.

At the time of the 1841 annual meeting of the British Association for the Advancement of Science, Richard Owen was already widely known as a brilliant

© Doug Henderson

***Iguanodon*, among the first dinosaurs ever discovered, roamed Europe in the Early Cretaceous.**

anatomist and paleontologist, and also as a cold and pompous man. He had carefully studied the fossilized bones of *Iguanodon*, *Megalosaurus*, and other recently unearthed creatures, all of which had been identified as huge versions of modern-day lizards, with lizardlike shapes and habits.

Owen, though, disagreed strongly with that classification. With characteristic straightforwardness (if not arrogance), he decreed that these creatures—and others that he had not yet studied—belonged instead to their own distinct group, which he called the *Dinosauria*, or "terrible lizards."

And so the dinosaurs were born, and so they have remained. Today, despite a slew of controversy, ongoing disagreements, and gaps in the record, we do have a

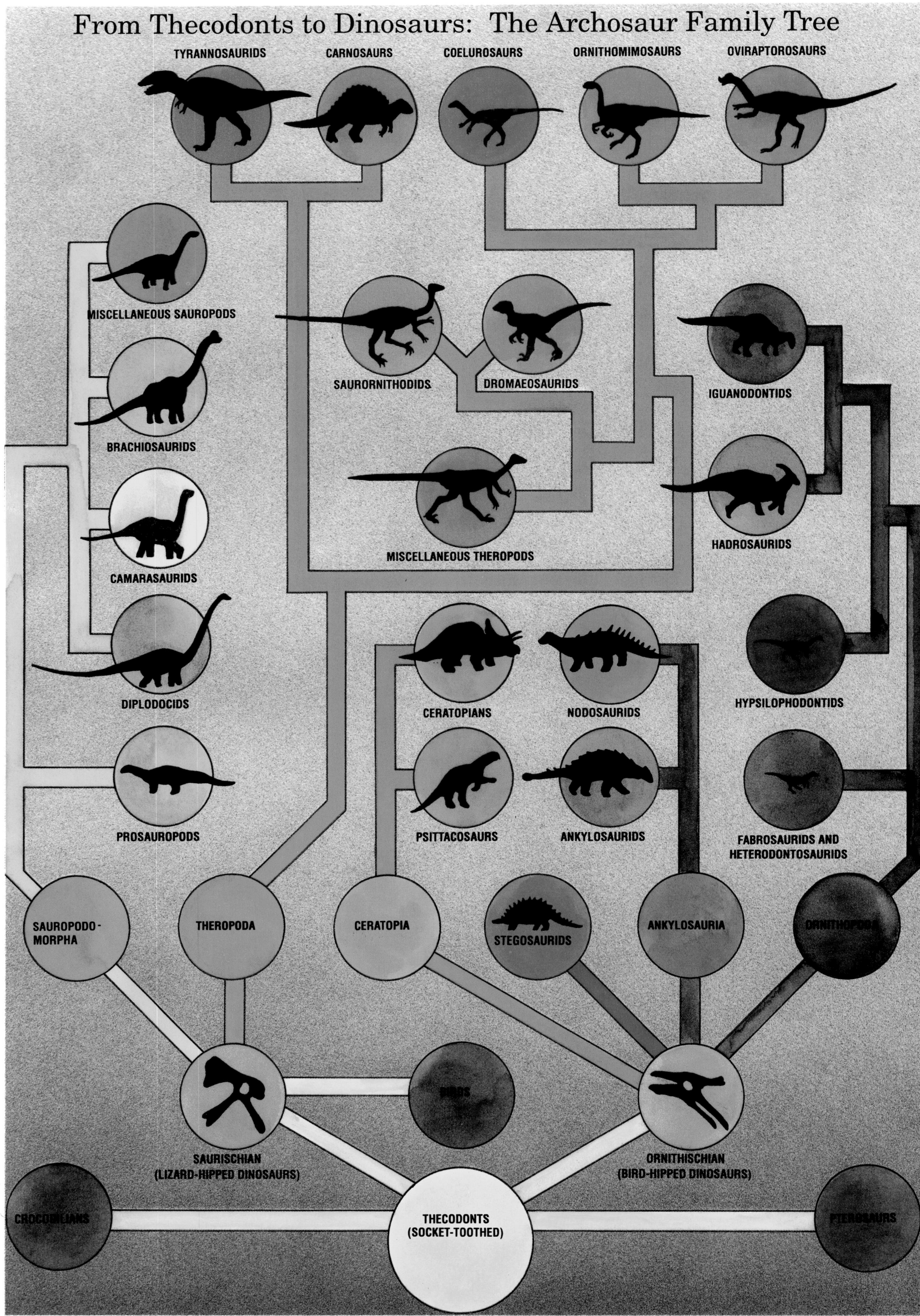
From Thecodonts to Dinosaurs: The Archosaur Family Tree
TYRANNOSAURIDS
CARNOSAURS
COELUROSAURS
ORNITHOMIMOSAURS
OVIRAPTOROSAURS
MISCELLANEOUS SAUROPODS
SAURORNITHODIDS
DROMAEOSAURIDS
IGUANODONTIDS
BRACHIOSAURIDS
MISCELLANEOUS THEROPODS
HADROSAURIDS
CAMARASAURIDS
DIPLODOCIDS
CERATOPIANS
NODOSAURIDS
HYPSILOPHODONTIDS
PROSAUROPODS
PSITTACOSAURS
ANKYLOSAURIDS
FABROSAURIDS AND
HETERODONTOSAURIDS
SAUROPODO-
MORPHA
THEROPODA
CERATOPIA
STEGOSAURIDS
ANKYLOSAURIA
ORNITHOPODA
BIRDS
SAURISCHIAN
(LIZARD-HIPPED DINOSAURS)
ORNITHISCHIAN
(BIRD-HIPPED DINOSAURS)
CROCODILIANS
THECODONTS
(SOCKET-TOOTHED)
PTEROSAURS

King
Philip
Came
Over
From
Germany
Smashed

pretty strong idea of the general outlines of the classification of the great reptiles.

Dinosaur classification, like that of all creatures, follows a clear structure, beginning with the most general category (kingdom), and ending in the most specific (species). The whole ladder, starting at the top, is as follows: kingdom, phylum, class, order, family, genus, species. If you have trouble remembering the correct order of the classification, you might want to use this common mnemonic device: King Philip Came Over From Germany Smashed. Or you might want to invent your own.

Everyone agrees that the dinosaurs belong to the animal kingdom, and to the phylum Chordata, or animals with backbones. Nearly everyone also agrees that they fall into the class Reptilia, or reptiles, which they share with modern lizards, turtles, and crocodiles.

Now it gets a little more complicated. Normally, right below class would come order—but scientists have inserted another rung on the ladder (forget the mnemonic for a while). Depending on who you talk to, they call this rung a subclass or superorder, but they all agree that it contains a group named Archosauria, the "ruling reptiles." In addition to the dinosaurs, Archosauria encompasses such dinosaur ancestors as the thecodonts and pterosaurs, as well as such modern reptiles as crocodiles, alligators, and—amazingly—birds.

Below the subclass Archosauria is the most important classification so far, the one that provides perhaps the most crucial division in the dinosaur world. All dinosaurs, scientists believe, fall into one of two orders: *Saurischia*, lizard-hipped dinosaurs, and *Ornithischia*, bird-hipped dinosaurs.

The most basic difference between the two orders actually does have to do with the shape of their hips. All dinosaurs had three main bones in their hips, but the bones that were placed very differently in each group. In the Saurischian order, each bone pointed in a different direction, with the pubic bone usually pointing forward.

No matter what form of dinosaur you were, you have a place in the system of classification followed by modern scientists. Exactly what place you'd occupy, particularly in the busy and confusing Cretaceous, remains open for debate.

Ornithischian hip bones were shaped like those found in birds, with both the pubic bone and the ischium pointing backwards.

This seems like a subtle distinction, but scientists believe that these and other differing characteristics made the bird-hipped and lizard-hipped dinosaurs rather distant relatives. Certainly, as will be seen later in this chapter, the two orders evolved into dinosaurs that often barely resembled each other.

For now, however, let's follow the classification ladder down another rung. In the usual progression, what follows order is family—but that's not true in the complicated world of the dinosaurs. Among the saurischians, order is followed by two suborders: *Theropoda* (the great meat-eating dinosaurs and others) and *Sauropodomorpha* (including the plant-eating sauropods like *Apatosaurus*). Ornithischian dinosaurs are divided into four suborders: *Ornithopoda* (including the duckbills and many other odd dinosaurs), *Stegosauria* (plated dinosaurs), *Ankylosauria* (armored dinosaurs), and *Ceratopsia* (horned dinosaurs).

Is that relatively clear? Unfortunately, each of the saurischian suborders (*Theropoda* and *Sauropodomorpha*) are also divided into infraorders—but we won't go into that too deeply yet. Instead, we'll pick a single line, ending in one of the most famous of all dinosaurs, the great *Tyrannosaurus rex*.

Tyrannosaurus (like nearly all meat-eating dinosaurs) is a saurischian, belonging to the *Theropoda* suborder. It is also part of an infraorder, *Carnosauria*, which includes all of the largest meat-eaters. Its family is *Tyrannosauridae*, containing many dinosaurs similar to our subject. Next step on the ladder is the genus, which in this case is *Tyrannosaurus*. The individual species is *Tyrannosaurus rex*.

Notice that books and articles rarely call this dinosaur—or any other—by its species name. The number of species is too large and uncertain, and the differences between similar ones too slight to concern all

"Look out, Thak! It's a ... a ... dang! Never can pronounce those things!"

Gregory S. Paul/© World Book, Inc.

An animal, a reptile, an archosaur, a saurischian, a sauropod, an apatosaur—all describe this magnificent *Apatosaurus ajax*.

but the specialists. Therefore, we refer to all dinosaurs by their genus names: *Triceratops, Apatosaurus, Stegosaurus, Tyrannosaurus*.

To sum up, when you see the skeleton of a *Tyrannosaurus rex* in a science museum, you're looking at an animal, a reptile, an archosaur, a saurischian, a theropod, a carnosaur, a tyrannosaur, and a *Tyrannosaurus rex*—all in a single, huge package.

So what's all that about the warning at the beginning of this chapter? Where's the controversy?

I'll try not to disappoint you. Controversy can be found throughout the history of dinosaur classification. Some experts, for example, believe that the two saurischian suborders (*Theropoda* and *Sauropodomorpha*) are so dissimilar that they prove that *Saurischia* is an artificial order. Similarly, one characteristic of the ornithischians is that they are all plant-eaters—yet the recently studied *Tröodon* "Wound tooth" was clearly an ornithischian, but also a meat-eater. Do more such contrary dinosaurs wait to be found? And if so, what does this mean for dinosaur classification?

But no recent classification brouhaha has been greater than that created by maverick paleontologist Robert Bakker. With characteristic candor, Bakker has proclaimed that the very structure of the accepted classification system for dinosaurs is fatally flawed. In fact, he says, the flaws begin near the top of the ladder.

Bakker acknowledges that dinosaurs belong in the Animal Kingdom and that they have backbones—but that's about as far as he'll go. For he believes that scientists have long been incorrect in considering dinosaurs reptiles. Rather, he thinks that many of his well-known theories—especially that all dinosaurs were warm-blooded—as well as the knowledge that birds and dinosaurs were closely related, make it essential to remove dinosaurs from the reptile class and give them, and birds, a class of their own.

According to Bakker and Peter M. Galton, birds and dinosaurs should belong to a new class: *Dinosauria*. This would then be divided into three subclasses: *Saurischia*, *Ornithischia*, and *Aves*, containing the birds. And so, Bakker says, the dinosaurs would no longer suffer "guilt by association" by being lumped together with the sluggish, slow-moving, cold-blooded turtles, snakes, and other reptiles.

Not surprisingly, most other paleontologists have rejected this intriguing new classification system, just as many have rejected the idea that all dinosaurs had hot blood. But, right or wrong, Bakker and Galton have once again shown how fragile—and easily challenged—the supposed "facts" about these fascinating creatures will always be.

***Allosaurus*, one of the most powerful of all Jurassic predators, was also a prototypical carnosaur, the infraorder that also contained *Albertosaurus*, *Tyrannosaurus*, and other great meat-eaters.**

It doesn't look like much, but the difference in pelvic bone structure between bird-hipped (ornithischian) and lizard-hipped (saurischian) dinosaurs makes the two main branches of the dinosaur family tree only distant relatives.

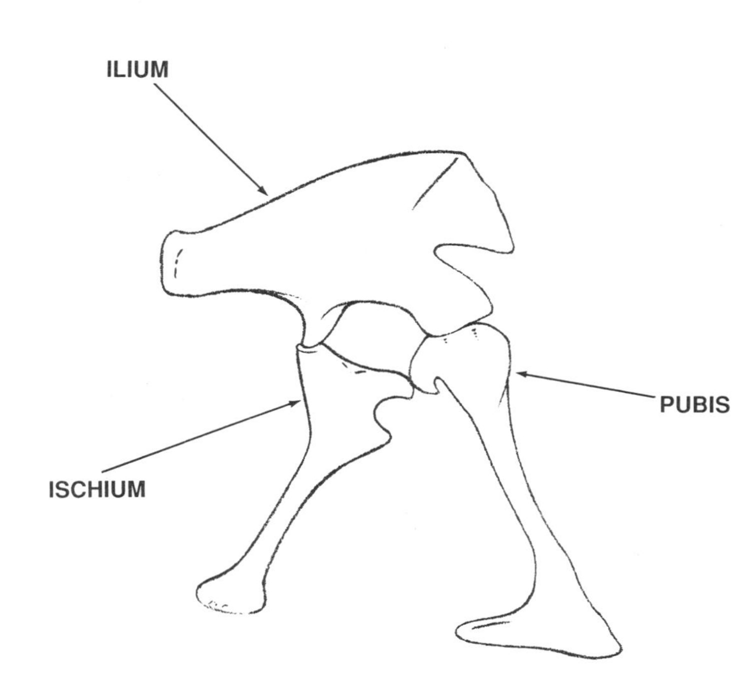

Saurischian Pelvis (Reptile)

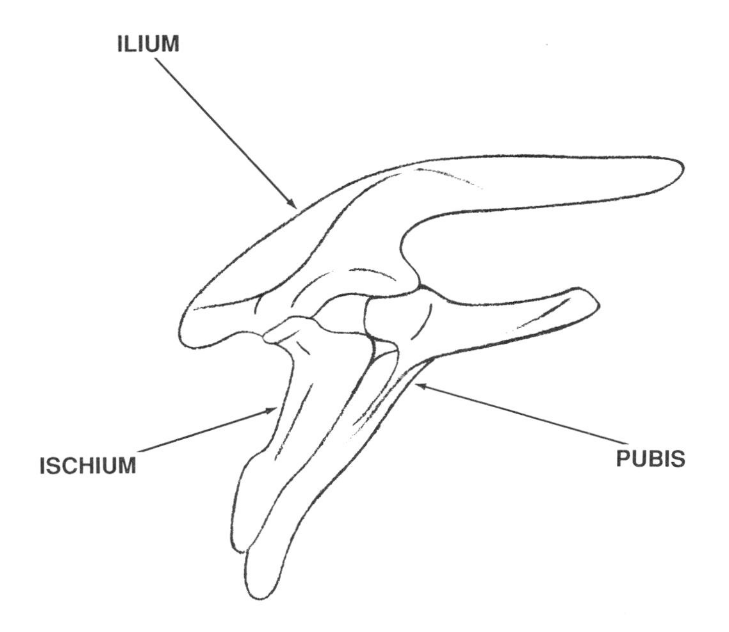

From the smallest to the most gigantic, every dinosaur was the end result of millions of years of evolutionary adaptation, perfectly suited to the warm, tropical environment that lasted through the Cretaceous.

DOUG
HENDERSON

Dinosaur Roots

Before we take an in-depth look at individual dinosaurs, it might be useful to survey the twelve (give or take a few) dinosaur suborders. What remarkable creatures they contained, how they evolved over time, and where they rose and fell during the reign of the ruling reptiles, makes a fascinating story.

Everyone agrees that the first dinosaurs evolved from a thecodont ancestor sometime during the Late Triassic. The question is: When was the Late Triassic? Older books will tell you that the first dinosaur appeared about 210 million years ago—but, like so much else in this ever-changing, revisionist history, the flood of discoveries during the past two decades has pushed the dawn of the dinosaurs much further back.

Today, most scientists agree that the earliest of all dinosaurs probably walked the earth about 225-230 million years ago. They weren't very common, most weren't very large, and they certainly weren't as varied as those of later years—but they were the first. And they included the prosauropods, an infraorder that saw both its flowering and its destruction in the earliest years of the dinosaur empire.

PROSAUROPODS
Order: Saurischia
Suborder: Sauropodomorpha

Because they disappeared so early, and because their fossil remains are scarce, the prosauropods are one of the least well-known groups of dinosaurs. And they varied so much that it's obvious we're missing most of the important information about them and their place in the dinosaur world.

We do know that many prosauropods were meat-eaters, including such fierce little hunters as the 10-foot

From dry grasslands and forested hills to humid swamps, the wonderfully diverse dinosaurs (including these *Edmontosaurus*) occupied every terrain on earth.

(3-meter) *Herrerasaurus* and the 6-foot (2-meter), scythe-toothed *Staurikosaurus*, one of the earliest known dinosaurs of all. Both of these odd dinosaurs—whose fossils are among the few ever found in South America—have characteristics resembling both the meat-eating theropods and the plant-eating sauropods.

Another group of prosauropods came closer to resembling the great sauropods (such as *Anatosaurus*) that thrived millions of years later. The *Plateosaurus*, for example, reached a length of 25 feet (7.7 meters), and had the sauropod's thick legs, long tail, and vegetarian habits. But it was a stumpy, short-necked creature, with none of the bizarre grace of its distant relatives.

The last prosauropods lived in Early to Mid Jurassic times. No one knows exactly why they died out, but the cause was most probably that they could not compete for food with the stronger, better equipped dinosaurs that arrived on the scene as the Jurassic period progressed.

SAUROPODS
Order: Saurischia
Suborder: Sauropodomorpha

Far better known and more spectacular than the prosauropods, this group of dinosaurs included the largest and heaviest animals ever to walk on land. Although there were at least five different families (which differed in skull structure, leg length, and other details), all sauropods shared these characteristics: a small head; a long, skinny neck; a huge, blocky body; columnlike legs; and a slender, tapering tail.

In habits, sauropods also resembled each other. All were plant-eaters. None moved particularly fast, although they were probably far more lively than depicted in early illustrations, which showed them as shambling, virtually comatose creatures. Most probably moved about in herds or family groups, with the young hiding in the center of the group where they were protected from predators.

Until relatively recently, scientists thought that

Like some, but not all, prosauropods, *Staurikosaurus* was an active hunter, using its large head and powerful jaws to attack smaller dinosaurs and other animals.

Although only an expert could identify this behemoth as a *Seismosaurus*, its long neck and tail, thick body, and trunklike legs clearly identify it as a sauropod.

sauropods spent most of their time lolling in the water, plucking up soft, floating vegetation and occasionally sinking below the surface like hippos, with only their nostrils (placed high on their foreheads) showing. Now, however, all those "facts" are considered to be wrong. Studies of the great reptiles' bone structure and teeth make it obvious that they lived on dry land, eating pine needles, tender shoots at the tops of trees, and other vegetation.

The earliest sauropods, including such individuals as the *Chinshakiangosaurus*, appeared at the very end of the Triassic and beginning of the Jurassic. They tended to be comparatively small (for sauropods, that is), reaching a maximum length of 40 feet (12 meters) or so. They were also far heavier-boned than their later kin.

As the Jurassic period progressed, the sauropods grew far larger and more diverse, reaching their greatest glory in the Late Jurassic. This was the era of the thick-necked *Camarasaurus*, the emaciated *Diplodocus*, and the vast *Seismosaurus*. Many of these common Late Jurassic sauropods lived in what is now North America.

Sauropods survived through the Cretaceous. But, unlike most other groups, they dwindled in size as time went on. For example, *Saltasaurus* was a typical Late Cretaceous sauropod, reaching 40 feet (12 meters) in length—about as long as the very first sauropods, and less than half the length of some Late Jurassic species.

Among the fiercest and most intelligent of dinosaurs, the coelurosaurs made their appearance in the Late Triassic. *Coelophysis*, a 10-foot (3-meter) predator that roamed the swamps and forests of North America, was one of the earliest.

COELUROSAURS
Order: Saurischia
Suborder: Theropoda

The coelurosaurs were a group of fleet-footed carnivorous dinosaurs that survived in increasing numbers and variety from the earliest dinosaur days through the Late Cretaceous. A few were as tiny as roosters, and all but the largest may have reached only 15 feet (4.6 meters) in length. But what they lacked in size, they made up for with a host of other fascinating characteristics, including speed, intelligence, and fierceness.

The earliest well-known coelurosaur was *Coelophysis*, a powerful, 10-foot (3-meter) predator that roamed Late Triassic North America. Typically, scientists have had great trouble finding fossil links between *Coelophysis* and its most likely descendants, such as the slender, sharp-toothed *Coelurus*, which lived in the Late Jurassic. Another Late Jurassic coelurosaur was *Archaeopteryx*, the famous feathered dinosaur-bird.

The Late Cretaceous saw the most fascinating of all coelurosaurs, including *Avimimus*, the large-eyed, big-brained "Bird Mimic" which may also have had weak wings that enabled it to fly short distances, and *Noasaurus*, a fierce, 8-foot (2-meter) hunter.

The skeletal similarities among coelurosaurs, the famed feathered dinosaur *Archaeopteryx*, and modern birds have led some scientists to believe that *Archaeopteryx* is the link between all reptiles and birds.

ORNITHOMIMOSAURS

Order: Saurischia
Suborder: Theropoda

The ornithomimosaurs were among the oddest of all dinosaurs: They were tall, almost painfully slender, with skinny tails, fragile arms, small heads, and toothless beaks. As a group, they are also known as the ostrich dinosaurs, and the name is appropriate; striding along the plains on their thin legs, scanning the horizon constantly for predators, they resembled ostriches or other large terrestrial birds. Their main defense must have been their speed, which few other dinosaurs could hope to match.

Although they may not have been abundant as their relatives to the west, these and other unusual dinosaurs (bottom row, left to right: *Coelophysis*, *Ornitholestes*, and *Anchisaurus*; top row, left to right: *Dilophosaurus*, *Hadrosaurus*, *Dryptosaurus*) roamed eastern North America until the very end of the great reptiles' reign.

Like so many other groups, the ornithomimosaurs appeared during the Jurassic, but reached their peak of diversity right at the end of the Late Cretaceous. Early examples, such as *Elaphorosaurus*, were somewhat stockier and less agile. The later type—including *Ornithomimus*, *Gallimimus*, and *Struthiomimus*—all followed a very similar body type. Ostrich dinosaurs were probably omnivorous, eating plants, eggs, insects—whatever they could find.

DEINONYCHOSAURS
Order: Saurischia
Suborder: Theropoda

The deinonychosaurs were an entire infraorder of dinosaurs that wasn't discovered until the 1960s. Almost immediately they proceeded to turn the world of dinosaurs upside down. Slender, agile, fast-moving creatures equipped with a fearsome array of weapons, the deinonychosaurs were also among the most intelligent of dinosaurs. Scientists think they used their brains and their weapons (which included stiletto teeth, strong hands tipped with sharp claws, and a specially adapted "switchblade claw" on each foot) to hunt in packs, taking on dinosaurs far larger than themselves.

Deinonychosaurs, which probably were descendants of the coelurosaurs, were Late Cretaceous dwellers in the northern continents. Largest of all—and perhaps the most frightening predator in all of dinosaur history—was 13-foot (4-meter) *Deinonychus*, while others included *Velociraptor* and *Dromaeosaurus*.

All scientists agree that the deinonychosaurs, with their speed and ferocity, have added a new dimension to our knowledge of dinosaur habits. Experts such as Robert Bakker, however, have gone even further, using these active hunters as evidence that many dinosaurs must have been warm-blooded. A cold-blooded creature simply wouldn't have had *Deinonychus*'s energy, Bakker points out, nor its quick reflexes and agility. Many agree

Like all Deinonychosaurs, 13-foot (4-meter) *Deinonychus* was one of the most efficient of predatory dinosaurs.

© Doug Henderson

This group of *Struthiomimus*, foraging in a Late Cretaceous forest, provokes an irresistible question: Were any dinosaurs odder than the ornithomimosaurs, or ostrich dinosaurs, with their slender necks and tiny heads?

with this conclusion, but an equal number disagree—and so we are confronted with another conflict that may not be resolved until a working time machine is invented.

CARNOSAURS
Order: Saurischia
Suborder: Theropoda

Far larger and more ponderous than the deinonychosaurs, the carnosaurs include many of the most famous dinosaurs of all time. Though the carnosaurs' exact lineage and ancestry remains clouded by the vagaries of the fossil record, paleontologists think that these meat-eaters may have descended from the coelurosaurs. Evidence suggests that the first carnosaurs appeared early in the Jurassic (or, just possibly, at the very end of the Triassic), millions of years after the appearance of the *Coelophysis* and other early predators.

Carnosaurs varied greatly in size, but nearly all were

large (20 feet [6 meters] or more), heavyset creatures with huge jaws and knifelike teeth. One of the most common early ones was *Megalosaurus*, a 30-foot (9-meter) meat-eater that lived in what is now Europe, South America, Asia, and Africa; although complete skeletons of this dinosaur are rare, it left countless footprints across the Jurassic landscape, particularly in England.

Two of the best-known carnosaurs are *Allosaurus*, which resembled *Megalosaurus* but grew to the length of 35 feet (11 meters) or longer, and the remarkable *Tyrannosaurus*, which was among the largest, heaviest, and most powerful carnivorous dinosaurs known. At 40 feet (12 meters) in length, standing nearly 20 feet (6 meters) high, and weighing 7 tons (6.3 metric tons),

Below: *Allosaurus's* powerful neck and jaw muscles and knife-sharp teeth were its best hunting tools. Unlike smaller predators, most carnosaurs had comparatively weak arms and hands, which they probably rarely used during an attack.

Left: Recent findings and theories about dinosaur speed, agility, and vivid coloration are all emphasized in this image, as a pack of *Allosaurs* attack a fleeing herd of sauropods.

© Tyrrell Museum

Above: *Dromaeosaurus*—here shown feasting on a pair of dead *Centrosaurs*—had exceptionally powerful jaws and huge teeth for its small size, making it an unusual (but still fearsome) deinonychosaur.

Tyrannosaurus was truly a nightmarish creature. But, it—and *Allosaurus* too—may have had a bark far worse than its bite. Some experts believe that these massive meat-eaters may have depended on carrion for their food, as they may simply have been too large and heavy to do much hunting on their own.

SEGNOSAURS
Order: Saurischia
Suborder: Theropoda

If you've read other dinosaur books, you've probably at least heard the names of most of the dinosaur families mentioned here. Now welcome the segnosaurs, members of a tiny infraorder named in 1980, after some bizarre fossils were unearthed in Mongolia. (Mongolia, you'll soon discover, is the clear winner in the Where-The-Oddest-Dinosaurs-Lived Sweepstakes.)

Segnosaurs were definitely Late Cretaceous meat-eaters, but they differed greatly from the coelurosaurs and the carnosaurs–in fact, they barely resembled any other saurischian dinosaur. For example, segnosaur hips had a pubic bone that slanted backwards, like an ornithischian dinosaur's, rather than forward, like a saurischian's. Similarly, their jaws had sharp teeth in the back, but none in the front. Instead, they had strong beaks, like many ornithischians but no other saurischians.

The best known of the three possible segnosaurs is *Segnosaurus*, which reached 30 feet (9 meters) in length. Its odd beak, other details of its bone structure, and the presence of web-footed tracks near its fossils, lead some scientists to think that *Segnosaurus* might have lived mostly in the water and eaten fish.

Below: All other dinosaurs gave way before enormous *Allosaurus* and other carnosaurs.

© Bob Walters

ORNITHOPODS
Order: Ornithischia
Suborder: Ornithopoda

This widely varied suborder (the largest group of

bird-hipped dinosaurs) rose in the Late Triassic or Early Jurassic, but reached its peak in the Cretaceous, when it contained many of history's most abundant (not to mention bizarre) dinosaurs.

With just one exception, all ornithopods ate plants; many had strong grinding-teeth on the sides and back of their jaws, but only a powerful, toothless beak in the front. Most were well equipped for walking on their muscular hind legs, which they used to flee from any danger they spotted with their sharp eyes. Even so, ornithopods (particularly the larger, later ones) must have served, like wildebeeste do in Africa today, as easily caught meals for local predators.

The earliest ornithopods were almost certainly the fabrosaurs, small, primitive dinosaurs that roamed the earth in the Late Triassic and Jurassic. *Fabrosaurus*, a lightweight dinosaur that barely reached a length of 3 feet, 4 inches (1 meter), was a typical example. Many scientists believe that the fabrosaurs may have been the first of all ornithischian dinosaurs.

A little later on (perhaps fifty million years), the ornithopod family tree gave rise to the hypsilophodonts, which were among the speediest of all dinosaurs. The largest (such as *Dryosaurus*) reached a length of about 10 to 14 feet (3 to 4 meters), but all were slender, with racehorse-like legs and long, stiff tails they used for balance while running.

The most famous of all ornithopods—and the dinosaur whose tooth was found along an English roadside by either Gideon or Mary Ann Mantell in 1822 (see page 173)—was the Early Cretaceous *Iguanodon*, whose size and heft were harbingers of ornithopods to come. Reaching 30 feet (9 meters) in length, weighing as much as 5 tons (4.5 metric tons), *Iguanodon* must have shambled along, pulling succulent leaves from nearby trees and chewing them up with its ridged cheek teeth.

But if *Iguanodon* has retained a measure of fame, no ornithopods have become more beloved of scientists than

A typical duckbill in shape and size, *Maiasaura* was anything but typical in its nesting, breeding, and rearing habits.

its descendants, the hadrosaurs or duckbills. These large Late Cretaceous reptiles, perhaps the most common and widespread of all dinosaurs, boasted remarkable crests (shaped like mittens, hatchets, or unicorn horns), flaps of inflatable skin on their faces, and other hard-to-explain features. If that wasn't interesting enough, *Maiasaura* (and almost certainly other duckbills) raised, protected, and fed its children—a very unreptile-like habit. (For more information on dinosaur behavior, see page 57.)

PACHYCEPHALOSAURS

Order: Ornithischia
Suborder: Pachycephalosauria

Spot the *Pachycephalosaurus*, yet another of the remarkable dinosaurs that roamed western Canada during the Late Cretaceous. Hint: It has a domed head and a wistful expression.

Some scientists think that these dinosaurs belong in the same group as the ornithopods, but others believe

they were strange enough—and different enough—to warrant a suborder of their own. Reaching their peak in the Late Cretaceous, and living almost exclusively in North America, these dinosaurs didn't share the duckbills' odd crests and flaps. Instead, they developed outstandingly thick and bony skulls, leading to their affectionate common name, the boneheads.

The earliest known bonehead, an Early Cretaceous individual that lived on the Isle of Wight, was named *Yaverlandia*. It reached about 3 feet (1 meter) in length, and its skull was just a little thicker than an average dinosaur's. At the other end of the spectrum, however, was *Pachycephalosaurus*, a Late Cretaceous model. The largest known bonehead, reaching 15 feet (5 meters) in length, this wonderful dinosaur had a skull 10 inches (26 centimeters) thick, covered with knobs and spikes.

© Doug Henderson

Above: The slow-moving *Stegosaurs* had little to fear from *Allosaurus* and other predators.

Opposite page, above: The very end of the Cretaceous saw the increasing abundance of many bizarre dinosaurs, especially such armored ones as *Euoplocephalus*.

Opposite page, below: No dinosaur suborder was more varied than the ornithopods, of which this *Dryosaurus* was an early example. Inhabiting Late Jurassic North America and East Africa, *Dryosaurus* may have been a neighbor to *Allosaurus*, *Stegosaurus*, and other familiar dinosaurs.

STEGOSAURS
Order: Ornithischia
Suborder: Stegosauria

Many early bird-hipped dinosaurs had small rows of bony knobs lining their backbone. But none took this adaptation as far as the stegosaurs, the plated dinosaurs that lived from Mid Jurassic to Late Cretaceous times, reaching their greatest abundance in the Late Jurassic. Heavy-bodied, with thick hind legs often far longer than their forelimbs, these four-footed plodders could not have hoped to run from marauding predators. Instead, they may have depended on the great plates that lined their back for protection. (This is controversial; some experts believe the plates were used to deflect or absorb warmth from the sun). Without a doubt, however, stegosaurs used their powerful tails, lined with sharp spikes, as a flailing weapon while under attack.

The largest—and most famous—stegosaur is *Stegosaurus* itself. At 30 feet (9 meters) in length and 2 tons (1.8 metric tons), it was a formidable plant-eater, roaming western North America as did so many other dinosaurs large and small.

This *Allosaurus*, intent on preying on an alert *Stegosaurus*, seems taken aback by the plated dinosaur's strong defenses.

ANKYLOSAURS
Order: Ornithischia
Suborder: Ankylosauria

Appearing later than the stegosaurs, these Cretaceous armored dinosaurs reinforced the theory that the best offense is a good defense. With short, thick legs and massive bodies—designed for stability, not speed—they had to be able to protect themselves against hungry carnosaurs.

And protection is what they got. No other dinosaurs could compete with the ankylosaurs for the strength and variety of their defensive weapons. All had tough bony plates imbedded in the skin of their backs, along with a network of tooth-breaking knobs, spikes, and ridges on their heads, necks, sides, backs, and tails. Only their belly may have been vulnerable—but flipping them over couldn't have been an easy task.

At 35 feet (11 meters), *Ankylosaurus* was the largest and best known ankylosaur. As well as the above-mentioned defenses, it came equipped with a huge mass of fused bone on the end of its tail. This club, swung with crushing force, must have discouraged even those predators intent on making a meal of *Ankylosaurus*.

CERATOPSIANS
Order: Ornithischia
Suborder: Ceratopsia

Yet another group of late-evolving, abundant, extraordinarily successful ornithischians, the ceratopsians (or horned dinosaurs) stripped away many

© Gregory S. Paul

Above: Among the most ornate of all horned dinosaurs, *Pentaceratops* featured five horns and a remarkable, enormous neck frill. Like *Triceratops* and other relatives, it may have traveled in herds.

of the defenses that made the ankylosaurs and stegosaurs such plodding creatures. Instead, the later ceratopsians developed an array of long, sharp facial spikes that they must have wielded as potent weapons.

Even the earliest horned dinosaurs first appeared during the Cretaceous period, with nearly all arriving during the Late Cretaceous. Primitive individuals like *Protoceratops* and *Bagaceratops* resembled their later kin in shape, but lacked fully developed horns and rarely grew beyond 6 feet (3 meters) in length. Their best defense must have been avoiding the notice of hungry predators.

Later species were far larger and more striking. Twenty-five-foot (7.5-meter) *Pentaceratops*, for example, had a huge neck frill (perhaps used more for heat exchange than for defense), and five horns. Even more dramatic was *Triceratops*, the 30–foot (9-meter), 6-ton (5.4-metric ton) ceratopsian that may have been the biggest of all. *Triceratops* had only three horns, but they may have been 5 feet (1.5 meters) long, and were certainly extremely sharp. Put this together with *Triceratops*' speed and strength, and the fact that it ran in great herds, and you have one of Late Cretaceous North America's most impressive dinosaurs.

Below: Shaped like tanks, often armed with long, sharp horns, *Triceratops* and other horned dinosaurs were walking warnings to *Tyrannosaurus* and all other nearby hunters: Don't Mess With Me.

© Smithsonian Institution

© Bob Walters

Opposite page: Eye to eye with a *Triceratops*. Peaceful vegetarians they might have been, but these horned dinosaurs were as strong and as impregnable as tanks.

The Earth: 200,000,000 years ago;

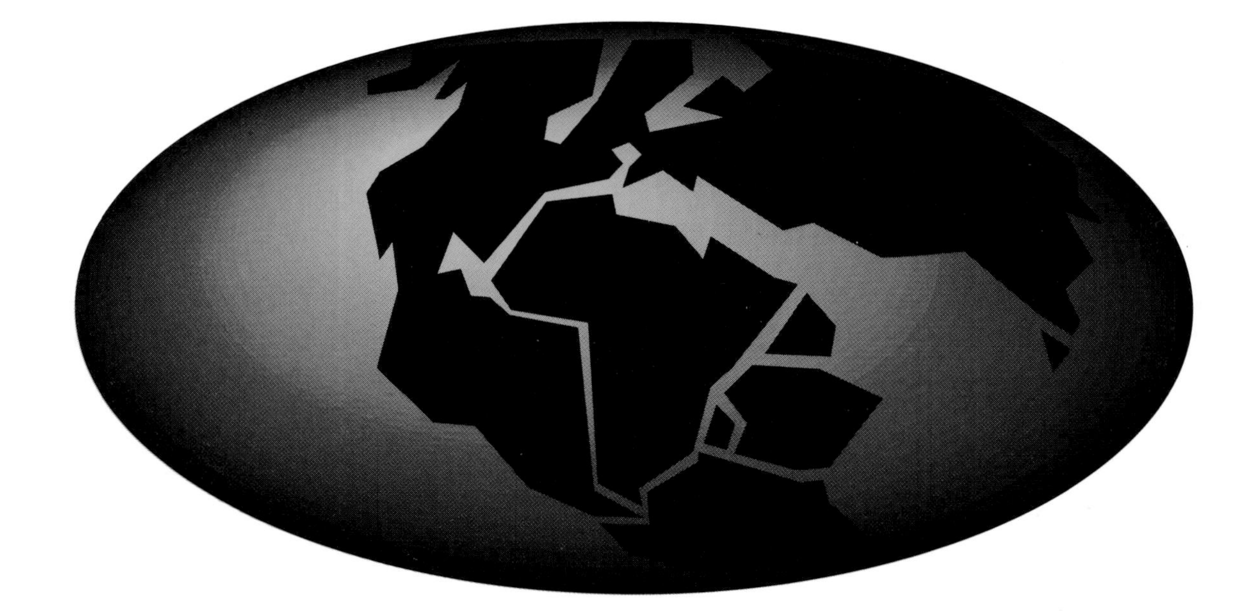

and now.

CONTINENTAL DRIFT:
Early in the dinosaurs' reign, the world was composed of one great continent called Pangaea. But the slow process of continental drift gradually carried the great land masses apart, until they reached today's familiar locations.

North Wind Picture Archives

Left: Say your prayers. The only thing that saved early humans from becoming meals for reptiles like this plesiosaur was a gap of tens of millions of years.

Below: Dinosaurs weren't the only fascinating reptiles occupying their ancient world. Take a look at this remarkable *Elasmosaurus*, an enormous plesiosaur that lived in Late Cretaceous oceans.

© Tyrrell Museum

© David Weisman

These Weren't Dinosaurs

A slew of books on dinosaurs appears each year, but one recent low-budget arrival has a particularly memorable theme. Its exact title escapes the mind, but it promises the inside story on dinosaurs of land, sea, and air. Why is that so funny? Because its author got only one of three right, and though a .333 batting average is great in baseball, its not so good in real life. Dinosaurs, as everyone knows, lived on land. What many people (including the author of that book) don't realize is that the great reptiles lived *only* on land. Nowhere else.

If a *Hadrosaur* fell off a cliff, it would—briefly—be a dinosaur of the air. If a massive sauropod stumbled into a deep bay of a wind-whipped inland sea and sank beneath the surface, it might justifiably be called a dinosaur of the sea.

But living, healthy dinosaurs, dinosaurs that knew what they were doing, were satisfied to be the dominant creatures on the vast continents of the Mesozoic era. The air and sea they left to other animals, a remarkable assemblage of giant flying reptiles and vast swimming reptiles that were as fascinating as the dinosaurs themselves. But they were not dinosaurs.

So what were they? The animals that were the most powerful hunters in the great seas were (like all reptiles) descendants of early amphibians that had struggled from the water millions of years earlier. From the Triassic onward, these reptiles returned to the oceans and lakes, which they found populated by enormous numbers of fish and amphibians. With such a wide-open food supply, the sea reptiles soon proliferated, growing to great proportions and taking on bizarre forms.

Among the most successful of all Triassic reptiles were the icthyosaurs, which may have a reached a length of 30 feet (9 meters) or more at a time when few dinosaurs were more than 10 feet (3 meters) long. These huge fish eaters are classic examples of parallel evolution: They were clearly reptiles, yet in form and behavior they resembled modern dolphins. With their streamlined shape, powerful flippers, and long, sharp jaws lined with knifelike teeth, they were (like dolphins) formidable predators.

Sharing the rich oceans with the icthyosaurs were the plesiosaurs, who evolved in a different direction. Plesiosaurs had large, blocky bodies, tipped with flat flippers. But their most dramatic feature was a long, versatile neck—a neck like that of the Loch Ness monster, which will certainly prove to be a surviving plesiosaur. If it exists.

The Jurassic saw the heyday of the swimming reptiles. Early on, some icthyosaurs reached astounding sizes, up to 50 feet (15 meters) in length. Then they were gradually replaced by enormous plesiosaurs, which spanned 40 feet (12 meters) or more. But by the end of the middle of the Cretaceous, all of these great sea monsters were declining and disappearing.

They were replaced at first by the enormous mososaurs, which looked much like gigantic lizards with flippers. By the end of the Cretaceous, however, all these ocean-going reptiles were dead or dying, victims of the great extinction that capped the Mesozoic era. Their replacements were smaller, less dramatic, but far more familiar: sharks, other large fish, and—eventually—whales and dolphins.

The huge flying reptiles called pterosaurs that ruled the air during the Mesozoic descended (as did the dinosaurs) from the thecodonts. But they weren't any more closely related to the dinosaurs than were the crocodiles, and were actually much further removed from dinosaurs than are today's birds.

Pterosaurs first appeared during the Jurassic. All had leathery wings, sharp claws, and long jaws equipped with sharp teeth. They shared other features with modern birds: hollow, lightweight bones, a strong breastbone for anchoring wing muscles, and large eyes.

Early species were rather small, with the tiniest being no larger than a pigeon and few possessing a wingspan greater

Throughout the dinosaurs' reign, the vast, turbulent oceans were dominated by huge marine lizards, while pterosaurs soared across the skies on leathery wings.

© Smithsonian Institution

Ranging from pigeon-sized to monsters with wingspans of 35 feet (10 meters), the pterosaurs were as dominant in the Mesozoic skies as dinosaurs were on land.

than 3 or 4 feet (90 centimeters to 1.2 meters). By the Cretaceous, however, many pterosaurs had grown to enormous size. The largest had a wingspan greater than 40 feet (12 meters) in length, yet its body may have weighed only a few ounces. Like a frigatebird or albatross, this huge reptile must have been a wonderfully delicate, graceful flyer, spending hours—or days— at a time aloft.

By the Late Cretaceous, true birds were becoming far more common, filling niches previously occupied by the pterosaurs. Like the dinosaurs, the swimming reptiles, and so many other animals, the last of the great flying lizards died out at the end of the Cretaceous. It's sad to think we ll never get to see one of those great, leathery beasts soaring across the prairie sky.

© Doug Henderson

© Doug Henderson

Dinosaur Behavior

© Gregory S. Paul

Above:This painting of a hyperactive *Dilophosaurus* is a perfect example of how most scientists now believe that dinosaurs were agile, fast-moving creatures.

Opposite page, above: *Maiasaurs* were caring parents, but had few defenses if attacked by the powerful carnosaur *Albertosaurus*.

Opposite page, below: By studying the remains of *Orodromeus* nesting areas at his Egg Mountain digging site, Jack Horner is learning much about the lives of these Cretaceous hypsilophodonts.

At first glance, the study of dinosaur behavior seems like an awfully unpromising field. After all, how rewarding can it be to study the habits, quirks, and nuances of creatures that have been dead for millions of years, and that exist today only as fossil relics?

But for Jack Horner, Robert Bakker, and many other paleontologists, the study of dinosaur behavior is not only possible—it's a vibrant, fruitful area that provides us with crucial insights into the lives of the great reptiles. In fact, Horner hosted an international symposium at the Museum of the Rockies in late 1988, whose entire purpose was to discuss recent findings and theories relating to the behavior of dinosaurs and other extinct animals.

Scientists researching dinosaur behavior use the fossil record in fascinating ways. To most of us, a skeleton only gives a sense of what the dinosaur looked like. But to the trained eye of a paleontologist, the same skeleton tells a far more detailed story. A dinosaur's teeth quickly show whether it ground fibrous vegetation between thick molars or tore flesh with sharp incisors. Similarly, its backbone provides clues to its posture, allowing us to determine whether it ran quickly on two legs or plodded along on all fours.

Close study of dinosaur skeletons, using powerful x-rays such as the CT scan, has also contributed to such ongoing disputes as whether the great reptiles were warm- or cold-blooded. Dinosaur bones are riddled with haversian canals, passages that carry blood through the bone. Mammals and birds, which are warm-blooded, have these passages—but the cold-blooded modern reptiles don't. "Dinosaur bones have far more haversian canals than do bird bones," says Jack Horner. "With this

With increasing frequency, researchers are uncovering the nests of dinosaurs—though never in as pristine condition as is shown in this diorama.

and other findings, I think the dinosaurs must have been warm-blooded."

Some fossil evidence must be studied in less certain, more imaginative ways. For example, some dinosaurs have odd features that defy easy explanation. The boneheads had ridiculously thick skulls, many duckbills featured odd crests (often with their breathing passages running back and forth within), and the carnosaur *Centrosaurus* boasted an odd, seemingly useless little horn on its nose.

By comparing dinosaurs with modern animals, scientists have devised plausible explanations for many of the dinosaurs' oddest attributes. The boneheads' skulls may have been used in violent battles for dominance in a herd, with male dinosaurs banging heads in much the same way as bighorn sheep clash horns today. And duckbills' crests might have served as echo chambers, allowing the dinosaurs to produce loud honking sounds that helped keep a herd together or alerted them to approaching danger.

Other advances in our knowledge of dinosaur behavior depend on pure luck. The best example of this, of course, is the discovery by Jack Horner and Robert Makela of nesting grounds of the duckbill *Maiasaura*. Here they found concrete evidence that these dinosaurs cared for and fed their young. The luck in this case was twofold: eighty million years ago, a great ashfall killed the entire colony, and in the late 1970s the two paleontologists discovered the unique site. The further discoveries and brilliant deductions that followed the initial find, however, were far from just lucky.

While fossil skeletons have given us great insights into dinosaur behavior, trackways may hold even more

Superstar of parental care among the dinosaurs, *Maiasaura* fed and protected its growing young for a period of weeks or months, much as birds do today.

valuable clues. Studying the distance between the fossilized footprints of several dinosaur genera, and comparing them to the dinosaur's bone structure, British paleontologist R. McNeill Alexander devised a formula to pinpoint how quickly the reptiles moved.

What he and other scientists found was that many dinosaurs were far speedier than we ever imagined. The meat-eating *Velociraptor*, for example, was as fast as a racehorse, reaching speeds as great as thirty-five miles per hour (fifty-six kilometers per hour), while even the great sauropods plodded along at four or five miles (six or eight kilometers) per hour. Thus, another dinosaur myth—the one about how slow and unwieldy the great reptiles were—was forced into retirement.

Trackways also reveal a great deal about the habits of everyday life among the great reptiles. For example, *Triceratops* trackways frequently show large numbers of the horned dinosaurs heading in the same direction at the same time. This tells scientists that *Triceratops* (as well as *Maiasaurs* and other plant-eating dinosaurs) ran in great herds. Many also probably migrated seasonally in search of food, as do today's wildebeest in Africa.

Some sauropods also traveled in herds or family groups, footprints tell us, although probably not in groups as large as *Triceratops*. Even more interestingly, trackway patterns indicate that the sauropods traveled in a structured group, with adults stationed on the periphery and juveniles in the center of the herd. In this way, the young may have been protected from attack by *Allosaurus* or other predators.

Sauropods were just one subject discussed at the international symposium at the Museum of the Rockies. Argentine paleontologist Rodolfo A. Coria reported on some recent fossil finds of *Patagosaurus*, a Patagonian sauropod. Two adults and three juveniles apparently died at one time; the presence of the juveniles, which were of varying sizes, provides concrete evidence of prolonged parental care—another blow to the ages-old theory that dinosaurs didn't care for their young.

Other details of dinosaur behavior revealed at the symposium included further insights into the diversity of armor among ankylosaurs (they may have used their spines and plates to intimidate predators, not only to defend themselves); new evidence that the great *Tyrannosaurus* did hunt living prey (a duckbill skeleton contained a partially healed backbone that could only have been bitten by a large carnosaur, probably *Tyrannosaurus*); and a fascinating analysis of limb length among plant-eating dinosaurs by Christine Janis of Brown University in Rhode Island. According to Janis, Late Cretaceous climatic changes may have reduced available vegetation, forcing the dinosaurs to wander widely in search of food. This struggle to survive is echoed in gradually increasing limb lengths among many plant-eaters.

"I believe that, with enough time, we can learn a tremendous amount about how the dinosaurs lived," says Jack Horner. If the above findings are any indication, there is little doubt that he's right.

> To be honest, I really don't care what killed the dinosaurs.
>
> — Jack Horner

A likely extinction scenario: Following vast environmental changes, the plant-eating dinosaurs starved, providing a feast for these *Dromaeosaurs* and other predators. Soon enough, though, the bounty was gone, and the meat-eaters, too, marched into extinction.

Off To Theory Heaven: *The Death of the Dinosaurs*

For Jack Horner, the questions surrounding the reptiles' extinction are little more than a distraction. He and many other paleontologists are far more interested in piecing together the fascinating puzzle of dinosaur behavior, an effort that has in recent years revealed spectacular insights into the dinosaurs' breeding, feeding, and hunting strategies. "I think there's a lot more to learn about the way dinosaurs lived than about how they might have become extinct," agrees paleontologist Mick Hager.

But despite these lonely voices of reason, most experts and amateur dinosaur enthusiasts remain entranced by the death of the dinosaurs. After all, these were the biggest, most powerful, most abundant, and longest-lived animals ever to stride across the ancient plains, hills, and mudflats. They thrived for far longer than any other class of animal in the earth's history. They were so adaptable that they filled a number of ecological niches; from tiny, skulking plant-eaters to great predators, the dinosaurs were everywhere.

Then they died. Disappeared. Vanished from the face of the planet, along with the pterosaurs, plesiosaurs, and countless other animals. As soon as the first nineteenth century scientists pronounced that a race of giant reptiles had once lived where London now stood, it became clear that these were extinct creatures, that (unless one or two still lived in dense African or South American jungles) every last *Tyrannosaurus* and *Triceratops* was gone forever. The next question—and one that people have been asking ever since—was *Why*?

Early on, scientists discovered new evidence that made the extinction puzzle even tastier. At the very end of the Cretaceous period, about sixty-five million years ago, dinosaur fossils were still found in relatively large numbers. But in rock dating from the very beginning of the Tertiary period that followed, experts could find no solid evidence that any dinosaurs had survived. Somewhere in the transition between the two periods (known as the K-T Boundary), the dinosaurs died out.

Of course, they weren't the first animals on earth to pass on. Extinctions have occurred throughout history, and the passage of time has claimed far more species than currently survive. But the dinosaurs' very success makes their extinction more interesting than most. Plus, people are fascinated by dinosaurs, and intrigued and frightened by death. So the death of the dinosaurs is a guaranteed smash hit.

About a day after the dinosaurs were "discovered," scientists began developing theories as to how the great reptiles became extinct. Many of the earliest theories now look naive, even ridiculous, but it's important to remember that experts are still arguing over wildly contradictory theories—and the question will probably never be answered to everyone's satisfaction.

What follows is a partial listing of theories popular through the ages, starting with some of the first and most entertaining and running through those that make paleontologists growl at each other today.

A far less likely extinction scenario, although only a shade more unbelievable than some proposed by reputable scientists.

THEORY: *The dinosaurs died out because, as a race, they became senile and forgot how to breed and find food.*

DISCUSSION: This was a popular early theory, based on the belief that animal species follow the same progression that individuals do: youth, maturation, and gradual decline. Therefore, by the time the dinosaurs had been around for a hundred million years or so, they must have been getting pretty old—so old that they simply couldn't survive any longer.

Those proposing this theory pointed to certain fossil evidence as proof that the dinosaurs had been sliding into decay. For example, they said, glandular malfunctions in the brain resulted in the admittedly wild and unorthodox neck frills of Late Cretaceous horned dinosaurs and the bizarre crests adorning so many duckbills. Thus, they deduced, dinosaur senility.

Is it necessary to add that this theory quickly fell out of favor from the lack of any real evidence—not to mention general silliness?

THEORY: *Dinosaurs grew to be too large, and were no longer able to support their great size with enough food. Result: they starved to death.*

DISCUSSION: There's no doubt that as the Age of Dinosaurs stretched on, the general trend among the great reptiles was toward greater size. *Tyrannosaurus* was indeed the biggest carnosaur of all, and no other horned dinosaur exceeded *Triceratops*' length. Yet there was simply no fossil evidence that these dinosaurs had grown "too" big, and they apparently got around fine. (In fact, great herds of *Triceratops* may have roamed hundreds of miles in search of food—not the behavior of an animal too large for its own good). Also, plenty of smaller dinosaurs and many other animals and plants also died out along with the large dinosaurs.

A variation on this theory suggests that the dinosaurs' spines weren't able to support their great bulk, and that the resulting disk problems prevented the reptiles from finding food or mating successfully. Although this scenario is quite believable to anyone who has ever had a bad back, it's not supported by the facts.

THEORY: *Dinosaurs were simply too stupid to survive.*

DISCUSSION: Come now. Senile, stupid, too fat—was there anything the dinosaurs did right, except live 160 million years?

This theory gained quick popularity as soon as people realized that the dinosaurs had very small brains relative to their body size. Some, like the sauropods and armored dinosaurs, had almost comically tiny heads that couldn't have contained a brain much larger than a tennis ball. No one has ever attributed great intelligence to these or other dinosaurs.

But stupidity so great that it killed them? No way. It's typical of humans to consider every other creature on earth as barely capable of surviving its own dimwittedness, but we have to remember, once again, that the dinosaurs were among the most adaptable and successful animals in all of history. Their brains may not have allowed them to compose a symphony or write a best-seller, but the great reptiles were smart enough to live an awfully long time. And if they weren't smart enough to outlive whatever killed them off, we can't blame their brain size; alligators and many other creatures with small brains survived the great extinction with little trouble.

THEORY: *The arrival of flowering plants during the Cretaceous period doomed the dinosaurs to extinction.*

DISCUSSION: This theory is still held by some reputable scientists, and it's certainly more intriguing than those above. Flowering plants, grasses, and trees did indeed make their first appearance in the Cretaceous, more than 100 million years after the dinosaurs arrived. And, as we now know, many species of flowering plants contain poisonous chemicals known as alkaloids, which in large enough doses can kill a plant-eating animal.

Most animals avoid these poisonous plants. But, the theory goes, dinosaurs had no prior experience with alkaloids, and weren't able to taste their bitterness. So they gorged themselves on poison, and died out.

This theory is unprovable, one way or the other. But a strong piece of evidence argues against it: Flowering plants appeared more than 100 million years ago, or about forty million years before the dinosaurs disappeared. It is unlikely that the great reptiles' death throes would have lasted that long. "At most," says paleontologist Nicholas Hotton, "alkaloids must have just been minor contributors to the dinosaurs' extinction."

Could a catastrophic supernova—the enormous explosion of a nearby star—have rained deadly radiation on the dinosaurs? Scientists think not, but may never agree on what did happen.

Dinosaurs, like this placid *Edmontosaurus*, were perfectly suited to their warm, food-rich environment. But they may have been unable to adapt to colder weather that killed off many types of plants.

THEORY: *Mammals doomed the dinosaurs by eating their eggs.*

DISCUSSION: This theory, also unsupported by any evidence, has lasted a long time. This is probably because those who believe in it are sore about one simple fact: The mammals were, without doubt, an inferior, unimportant class of animals during the reign of the dinosaurs. Some existed when the dinosaurs first arrived, and some existed when the dinosaurs died out. But they never got much larger than rats, and all were skulking creatures that the dinosaurs rarely, if ever, noticed.

Yes, mammals probably did eat dinosaur eggs. At his Egg Mountain hypsilophodont nesting site in Montana, Jack Horner has unearthed fossils of early mammals, alongside those of several dinosaurs and other ancient reptiles. "The mammals must have eaten whatever they could find," he says. "I'm sure they nibbled at the hypsilophodont eggs, but there's no chance they did any significant damage." Without a doubt, the same held true elsewhere.

One by one, each of these theories, blaming the dinosaurs themselves or some other living things for the great reptiles' extinction, was discredited. Yet the dinosaurs did die out, and their death was seemingly both quick and brutal. So paleontologists, frustrated by their inability to find proof (or at least devise a believable scenario), began to look for some greater cause, some vast cataclysm that could neatly explain how such successful creatures could disappear so rapidly. A few of the most popular ideas follow.

THEORY: *The dinosaurs were destroyed when the earth's magnetic poles reversed polarity, allowing deadly cosmic radiation to bombard the earth.*

DISCUSSION: One of the wonderful things about the study of dinosaurs is that many things that sound ridiculous may contain a grain of truth. For unknown reasons, the earth's magnetic poles do change their polarity; three-quarters of a million years ago, compass needles would have pointed south. In addition, the magnetic field does act as a shield protecting the earth from deadly radiation. Experts believe that polarity reversals may have happened during the Late Cretaceous.

This is all very well, but the basic question remains: Did it cause the great extinction of the dinosaurs, pterosaurs, plesiosaurs, and others? Unfortunately, the answer is: We don't know. But it seems unlikely, for why would a reversal during the Late Cretaceous cause such widespread extinctions when the many that occurred before and since had a far less drastic effect?

THEORY: *A nearby exploding star, or supernova, rained deadly radiation down on the earth, spelling doom for many inhabitants, the dinosaurs included.*

DISCUSSION: Unlike the magnetic-reversal theory, this scenario assumes that the event provoking the great extinction was a one-time thing. But it doesn't explain why so many creatures survived the deadly rain that followed the supernova.

THEORY: *A huge comet or asteroid collided with the earth, raising a cloud of dust that effectively blocked out the sun for months or years. As a result of the sudden cold and darkness, most plants died, followed by plant-eating animals and then meat-eaters. In a remarkably short time, the dinosaurs and many other creatures disappeared forever, the victims of an "asteroid winter" they were unable to cope with.*

DISCUSSION: If you've read about dinosaurs before, you know that this theory—though it sounds no more provable than the two above—is actually one of the most popular and controversial of all time. Nearly every paleontologist has an opinion, and loud conflicts about it have been more the rule than the exception at scientific meetings during the past decade.

What makes the impact theory such a hot topic, while the reverse-polarity and supernova scenarios are rarely discussed? The answer is simple: Someone found evidence that a massive extraterrestrial impact did in fact occur.

The man who uncovered the evidence was a scientist named Walter Alvarez—and he isn't even a paleontologist. A geologist, Alvarez was interested in magnetic reversals and how they showed up in ancient rock. His study site was in Italy, and his attention was focused on the rock laid down at the very end of the Cretaceous and the beginning of the Tertiary, the K-T Boundary.

© Gregory S. Paul

Chasmosaurus **and other Late Cretaceous dinosaurs were unable to withstand the environmental disaster that followed the fall of a comet or asteroid, according to the Alvarez impact theory.**

In examining this stretch of rock, Alvarez noticed something odd: Between the limestone of the Cretaceous and the Tertiary lay a narrow stripe of reddish clay. The clay was very different from the rock on either side, and had virtually no fossils of any type in it. Its presence was unexpected—and very strange.

When Walter Alvarez and his father, the late physicist Luis Alvarez, analyzed samples of the clay, they were stunned by what they found. The rock at the K-T Boundary contained an enormous quantity of iridium, a rare element usually found only deep in the earth's core. Yet there it was, in quantities thirty times as great as those found in the rock above and below it. Researchers soon found that the layer of iridium-rich clay turned up nearly everywhere the K-T Boundary was studied, so the Alvarezes knew that some worldwide phenomenon must have been responsible. But what could it have been?

In 1980, the Alvarezes suggested a possible culprit: an enormous comet or asteroid, at least six miles (ten kilometers) in diameter, which had come crashing to earth at the end of the Cretaceous. Both comets and large asteroids are common in our solar system, and they do occasionally intersect earth's orbit at speeds of 60,000 miles (100,000 kilometers) per hour or more. Perhaps most importantly, they contain iridium, gold, platinum, and other elements at levels similar to those found at the K-T Boundary.

Ultimately, the Alvarezes' hypothesis was that sixty-five million years ago, a massive asteroid or comet slammed into the earth, probably into an ocean (explaining why no one has ever found the huge crater that must have resulted). The impact pulverized the extraterrestrial chunk, sending up an enormous cloud of iridium-rich dust, which quickly spread across the world, obscuring the sun.

For a period of several months following the collision, the earth was nearly dark, and plants on land and algae in the oceans, unable to photosynthesize, began to die.

What followed was a sudden, drastic period of global cooling, which killed off animals accustomed to warm climates and already weakened by lack of food. Chemical changes in the atmosphere may also have led to endless acid rainstorms, poisoning the lakes and oceans and killing plants on land.

Almost immediately, the theory said, many species would have been doomed. Only those lucky or adaptable enough to hang on until the dust eventually settled and temperatures returned to normal would have been able to greet the dawn of the Tertiary. For example, mammals, crocodiles, and many birds survived, but the pterosaurs, plesiosaurs, dinosaurs, and countless smaller creatures perished.

This was obviously a tremendously exciting and provocative scenario, and it shook the paleontological community like a bolt from above. At last, here was a hypothesis that was both plausible and testable, unlike those dealing with dinosaur "stupidity" or death by alkaloid poisoning. "The impact theory energized paleontologists throughout the world," Nicholas Hotton remembers. "Whether they initially believed it or thought it was rubbish, they went looking for evidence with more enthusiasm than ever before."

J. Keith Rigby, Jr., a geologist and paleontologist at Indiana's Notre Dame University, was one of the first experts to test the Alvarez hypothesis. Rigby and his assistants had already established an important Late Cretaceous dig along an ancient streambed in Hell Creek, Montana. As the impact theory began to gain popularity, Rigby realized that his findings at Hell Creek seemed to disprove the idea of a sudden, catastrophic dinosaur extinction.

The Hell Creek team had been charting Late Cretaceous dinosaur populations with a simple tool: the number of teeth found per ton of rock. "At the time of peak dinosaur populations, about thirty-five million years before the end of the Cretaceous, we find about two hundred teeth per ton," Rigby says. "Right before

© Doug Henderson

Although the ashfall that killed these *Maiasaura* took place millions of years before the death of all dinosaurs, scientists believe that the same cause—rampant volcanic activity—may have contributed to both the small and great extinctions.

the K-T Boundary, the number dwindles to about thirty teeth per ton."

But the most important number of all—and the one that casts the most doubt on the idea of a sudden, catastrophic extinction—is the number eighteen. That's the quantity of teeth found in rock that dates from hundreds of thousands of years *after* the K-T Boundary. These teeth, Rigby says, show conclusively that the dinosaurs didn't die out suddenly as a result of an asteroid winter at the very end of the Cretaceous, but declined gradually over the course of millions of years. In fact, the last dinosaurs survived well into the Tertiary.

Further evidence against the impact theory came recently from William A. Clemens, a paleontologist at the University of California at Berkeley. Clemens, a veteran of the Hell Creek fossil beds, more recently has been searching for—and finding—dinosaur remains in Alaska's North Slope.

Although these northern regions would not have been frozen during the mild, tropical weather of the dinosaurs' era, they would have experienced the months of near-darkness that characterize today's Arctic winter. If, as the impact theory states, dinosaurs died out largely because of the dust-driven unnatural darkness that followed the collision, how did these northern dinosaurs survive their yearly months-long dusk?

The Alvarezes and others who support the impact theory answered Rigby's and Clemens' findings by attacking their scientific ability, saying that both have misread the fossil evidence. But Rigby and Clemens are respected in the paleontological community, and most other experts believe that their conclusions are valid.

So, after all this, was there an impact or not? Nicholas Hotton believes that there was, and that it did affect the fate of the dinosaurs, but over a period of years, not months. Keith Rigby thinks there might have been a collision, but doubts it had anything to do with the great extinction. Robert Bakker and many others no longer believe that a comet or asteroid hit the earth at all.

But then, how do they explain the iridium at the K-T Boundary? And, more importantly, if there was no collision, how and why did the dinosaurs die?

Don't be disappointed, but the answer may lie in a theory far less dramatic than most of the above. It doesn't involve exploding stars, colossal impacts, or extraterrestrial objects of any kind. Instead, this theory centers on the natural changes the world and its climate were undergoing at the end of the dinosaurs' reign—changes that the great reptiles simply could not survive.

Dinosaurs, pterosaurs, plesiosaurs—all disappeared soon after the end of the Cretaceous. Only smaller creatures, like early damselflies, survived.

THEORY: *The end of the Cretaceous period was a time of tremendous upheaval on earth. All inland seas, which had existed for millions of years, dried up. The Rocky Mountains and other ranges rose. As the continents drifted away from the equator and toward the poles, the climate cooled, a cooling made more severe by the geologic facelift the world was undergoing. Volcanoes erupted everywhere, spewing molten rock from the core of the earth, polluting the air and, incidentally, creating the tell-tale iridium layer that has attracted so much attention in recent years.*

The dinosaurs had proven themselves remarkably adaptable animals—but even they could not withstand the environmental forces that gripped the Late Cretaceous. During the last thirty or forty million years of their reign, they declined in both number and diversity, eventually reaching a point where their numbers were simply too small to survive. A few lived on into the Tertiary, but by the K-T Boundary, the dinosaurs were doomed.

DISCUSSION: Without doubt, this theory (first put forth by geologists Charles Drake and Charles Officer in 1985) fits far better than any other with the concept of extinction as a natural, ongoing phenomenon. Nearly every living species in history has eventually become extinct, and almost always the cause has been its conflict with a more successful rival or its inability to adapt to a changing world.

Most paleontologists today believe that this is exactly what happened to the dinosaurs. The drier, cooler climate caused vast changes in plants, with many types disappearing and being replaced by others. Plant-eating dinosaurs may have found themselves without the foods they had depended on for countless generations; as their populations dwindled and disappeared, so did those of the great meat-eaters. A similar phenomenon occurred in the oceans, with a great die-off of algae and tiny organisms, followed by a wave of extinctions of larger animals, including the last great sea reptiles. Soon the world was a far emptier place than ever before.

But only for a few million years. For then, at the start of the Tertiary, an old, previously unimportant class of animals began to attain dominance. They were animals that had coexisted with the dinosaurs for more than 150 million years, but had never competed directly with the great reptiles. Now, after their long, patient wait, they were ready to conquer a world free of dinosaurs.

These animals? The mammals, of course.

The Age Of Mammals

Whether you buy the idea that the dinosaurs died in a sudden catastrophe, or tend toward the theory that the extinction was more gradual, you're likely to agree with one crucial point: The death of the dinosaurs put an end to the Mesozoic era like the crashing final chord of a symphony, leaving a world that must have seemed barren and unoccupied.

Yet it was also a world filled with opportunity. The dinosaurs had been so successful for so long that they had bulldozed all potential competition. By the end of the dinosaurs' reign, time had already passed other reptiles and amphibians by; they would never achieve dominance. Even mammals, adaptable creatures from the start, merely survived the endless reign of the dinosaurs. The mammals sniffing around the corpses of the last great reptiles were barely larger or more intelligent than those living millions of years earlier.

But now the dinosaurs were gone, and with them the Mesozoic era. Beginning sixty-five million years ago, and continuing today, is the Cenozoic era, or "time of recent life." The first, and longest, period of the Cenozoic was the Tertiary period, which lasted until a mere two million years ago. Today, the Tertiary is known as the Age of Mammals—and its course demonstrates beyond a doubt that, with the dinosaurs out of the picture, the mammals spread and diversified in fascinating ways.

Scientists have divided the Tertiary itself into five different epochs, in an attempt to impose order on a quickly changing world. The first epoch is called the Paleocene (meaning "ancient recent life") and stretched from sixty-five to fifty-four million years ago. During its span the world still looked very different from the way it looks today. Africa and Asia were discrete continents;

and though a narrow land bridge connected North and South America at the beginning of the Paleocene, it soon disappeared, leaving each a huge island.

For most of the epoch, the mammals resembled those of earlier times. It simply wasn't that easy to fill the niches left by the dinosaurs, so for perhaps ten million years, most mammals were small, shrewlike creatures that hunted insects and stayed out of sight. Had you been a visitor to this time, you would have found it impossible to believe that all ancient and modern mammals could have come from these unimpressive skulkers.

But by the end of the Paleocene, the process of adaptation was underway, and the mammals were taking on new forms and new roles. For example, condylarths, hoofed animals that were the earliest relatives of today's deer, antelopes, and cows, took a revolutionary step: They ate plants. As duckbills and other herbivorous dinosaurs had discovered, plants are tasty and easy to find, so the condylarths and other early plant-eaters flourished. Then, of course, so did such primitive carnivores as the creodonts, who thrived on the new abundance of meat.

Both plant- and meat-eating mammals continued to grow in size and diversity during the Eocene ("dawn of recent life") epoch, which spanned fifty-four to thirty-eight million years ago. From the most primitive condylarths sprang a variety of far more familiar ungulates (hoofed mammals), including the first rhinoceroses and tapirs and *Eohippus*, the hauntingly named "dawn horse." *Eohippus* was no larger than a small dog, but it was already well-adapted for running and eating grass—characteristics that have survived in horses to the present day.

The Eocene also saw the appearance of the first primitive whales and manatees, as mammals began to return to the oceans, just as icthyosaurs and other reptiles had done millions of years before. Early primates (resembling modern lemurs, like those still

Above: Not only the dinosaurs of Mongolia were spectacular and bizarre. This *Andrewsarchus* of the Late Eocene, for example, had a skull 3 feet (1 meter) in length. Scientists think it was a carrion-eater, tearing flesh and cracking bones with its powerful jaws.

Previous Page: A scene that must have been repeated countless times: *Smilodons*, or saber-toothed cats, attacking a wooly mammoth. The two were among the most common mammals in Pleistocene North America.

found on the isolated island of Madagascar) also evolved, the first in a long line leading directly to modern man.

Many spectacular animals populated the Oligocene epoch (the name, meaning "few recent epoch," refers to the number of modern creatures found then), which lasted from thirty-six to twenty-six million years ago. None were more spectacular than the titanotheres, large rhinoceros-like creatures that roamed North America before becoming extinct by the end of the Oligocene.

Other creatures remained abundant throughout the Oligocene, including early ancestors of today's cats, dogs, and pigs. The first truly apelike primates began to spread across Africa, while South America (at this time an island) harbored a host of odd, often gigantic sloths and other animals.

By the time of the Miocene epoch ("less recent epoch"), which lasted twenty-six to seven million years ago, the world was beginning to take on its present shape. New mountain ranges rose, including the Alps and Rockies, and the first polar ice caps appeared. India, long an island, joined with mainland Asia, although South America remained unconnected to any other landmass.

The Miocene was also a time of tremendous diversity among the world's mammals, with horses, antelopes, camels, and many less familiar animals living in great numbers on the grasslands of Africa and North America. The familiar saber-toothed cats made their appearance to hunt this easy prey, as did primitive wolves and others. The wildlife that characterized the Miocene must have been awe-inspiring.

During the Pliocene epoch ("more recent epoch") which lasted from seven to two million years ago, a land bridge finally connected North and South America, forging the last link in a chain of continental drift that saw the continents assume their present-day positions. This epoch was the final stage of the long Tertiary period; it saw a continuing evolution of primates and other mammals, as well as the disappearance of many

Above: No animal in history has had more impressive teeth than the *Smilodon*, whose huge upper canines were used for stabbing and slicing their prey—usually mammoths.

Below: Larger and shaggier than their modern relatives, mammoths were very similar in other ways to today's familiar elephants.

species. A visitor to the Pliocene would probably recognize most of the animals there, including bears, deer, and horses.

Scientists call the period ranging from two million years ago until just ten thousand years ago the Pleistocene epoch ("most recent epoch") of the Quaternary period, which followed the Tertiary and continues today. In geologic time, the Pleistocene occurred so recently and lasted so briefly that it's just the blink of an eye in the history of the world.

But it was a fascinating, vitally important period nonetheless. The Pleistocene saw the beginning of a long cooling trend in which as much as forty percent of the earth's surface was covered with glaciers. In fact, ice ages of varying strengths spread and receded across Europe, Asia, and North America throughout the two million years of this epoch; during the coldest stretches, so much of the earth's water was trapped inside glaciers that the levels of the oceans receded markedly. Some estimates put the oceans' depths as much as 500 feet (154 meters) lower than they are today.

This ebb and flow of ice had a dramatic effect on Pleistocene animals. Many were confronted by a disappearance of their lifelong food supplies. As a result, huge numbers of species died out, but others adapted and survived. Some species were forced to migrate south in search of food, leading to conflicts with species already living in these warmer regions.

Perhaps the most dramatic effect took place in South America, which until recently had been an island. Its native creatures, including giant ground sloths and others equally bizarre, had never before faced threats from outside, and were ill-equipped to defend themselves. Thus, the Pleistocene saw the extinction of many of the continent's most distinctive creatures, replaced by invaders from the north.

But the most important development of the Pleistocene had nothing to do with giant sloths, saber-toothed cats, woolly mammoths, or other treasures of

Opposite page: Larger brains and smaller jaws: The progression of the hominids, from *Australopithecus africanus* (2.5 to 3 million years ago) to *Australopithecus robustus* (1.75 million years ago) to *Homo erectus* (400,000 years ago) to *Homo sapiens neanderthalensis* (fifty thousand years ago), just a few steps from *Homo sapiens*, or modern man.

Below: Inhabiting western North America during the Eocene, both *Trogosus* and *Stylinodon* had strong, chisel-like front teeth, ideally suited for digging roots and tubers.

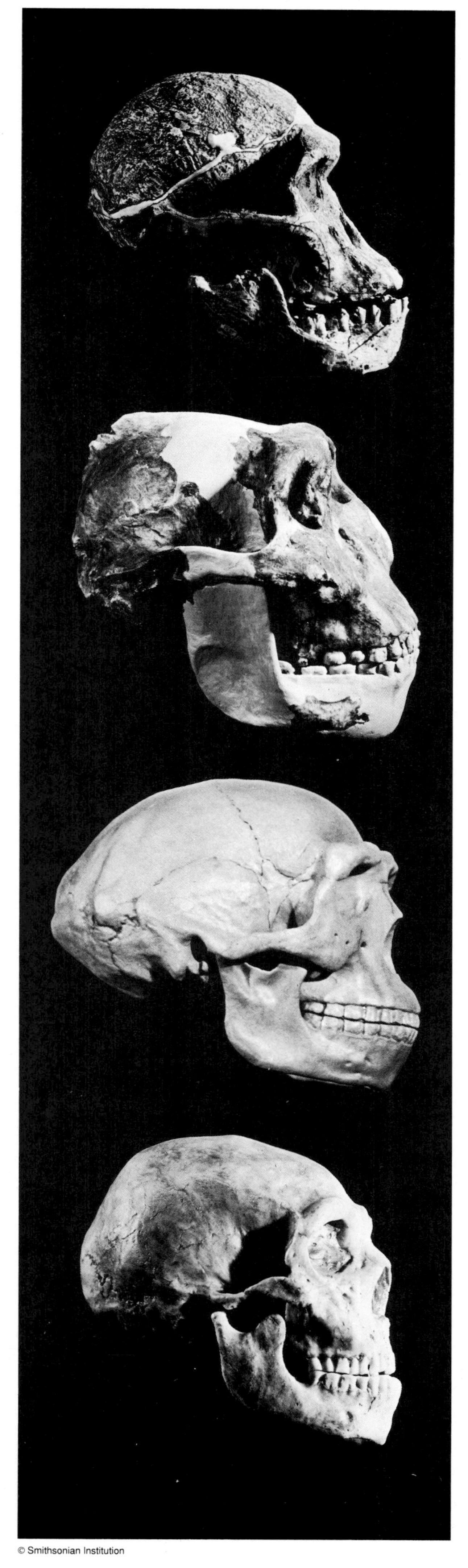
© Smithsonian Institution

the ancient world. No, it was a seemingly inoffensive, yet adaptable creature that left a greater mark on the earth than any other–even than the dinosaur. I'm referring, of course, to the hominids, the first primitive ancestors of modern humans.

Although scientists have long argued over the evidence, everyone agrees that the first human ancestor appeared, probably in Africa, during the Miocene epoch. *Australopithecus*, for example, was a comparatively advanced primate that lived in eastern Africa about two and a half million years ago, or about half a million years before the Miocene ended.

But it was the Pleistocene that witnessed the true rise of the hominids. *Homo habilis*, far more advanced than *Australopithecus*, seems to have arrived about two million years ago, while the first evidence of *Homo erectus* is dated about four hundred thousand years later. All of these hominids seem to have first appeared on the warm, game-rich plains of Africa.

More modern hominids continued to show up as the Pleistocene progressed, but the first *Homo sapiens* (our own species) didn't appear until about thirty-five thousand years ago. By this time, the hominids had spread to Asia and Europe, although they may not have reached North America until nearly the end of the Pleistocene, about eleven thousand years ago.

The last ice age lost strength about ten thousand years ago, and was replaced by a far warmer phase that scientists have dubbed the Holocene epoch ("recent epoch"), a warming trend that *Homo sapiens* welcomed by becoming the most dominant creature on earth since the dinosaurs. Everything we consider to be modern history has taken place during this stunningly tiny span of time, the briefest instant in the vast stream of life on earth. We need to dominate for another 160 million years before we approach the longevity of the great reptiles' empire.

PART 2

Dinosaurs A to Z

Gregory Paul 79

Dinosaurs A to Z

Key: *The dinosaurs in this section are color coded as follows:*

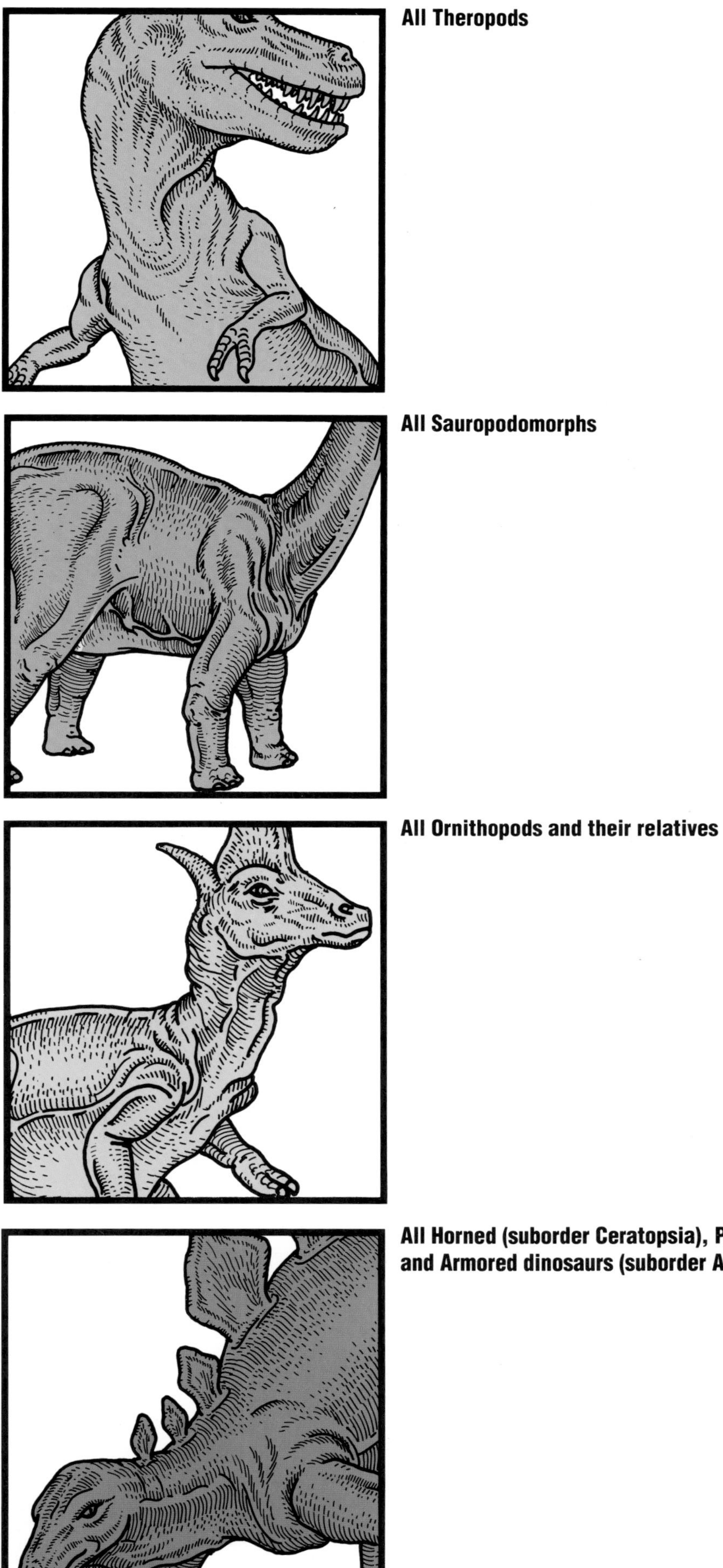

All Theropods

All Sauropodomorphs

All Ornithopods and their relatives

All Horned (suborder Ceratopsia), Plated (suborder Stegosauria), and Armored dinosaurs (suborder Ankylosauria)

Note: *The scale of the dinosaurs that appear in this section are approximate representations.*

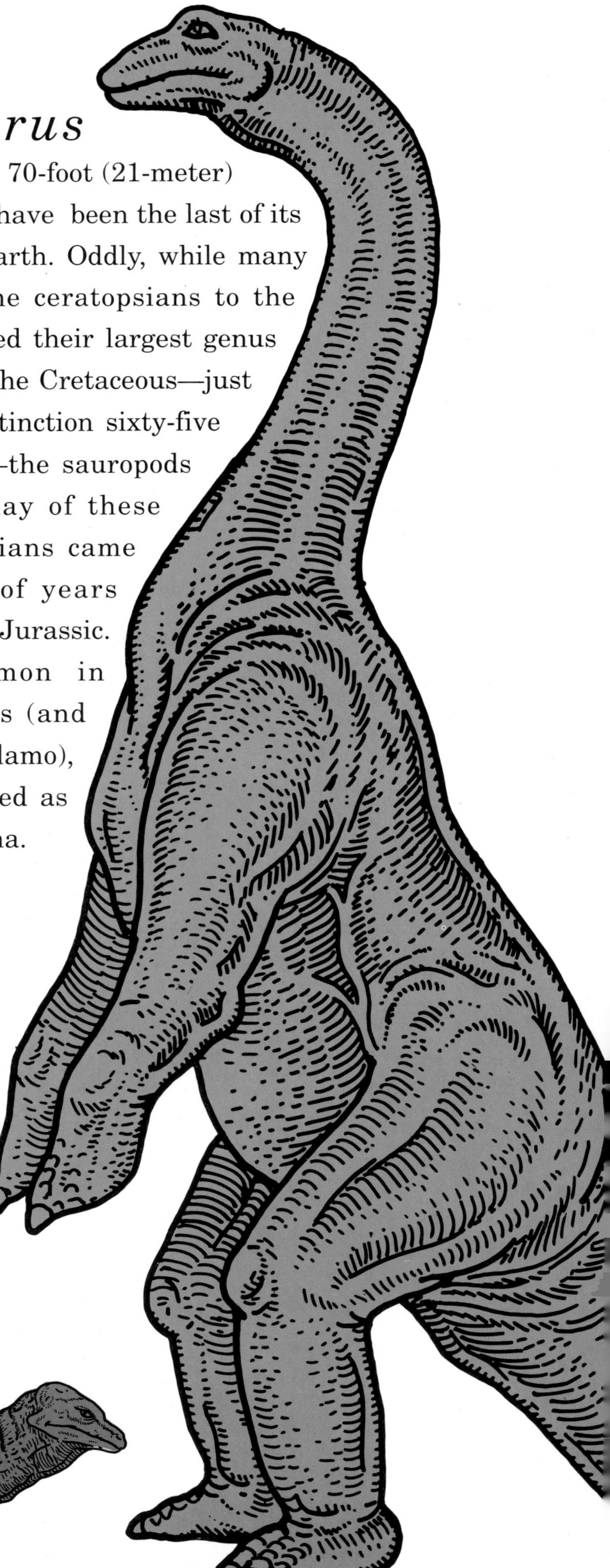

Alamosaurus

("Alamo lizard"). A 70-foot (21-meter) sauropod that may have been the last of its kind to walk the earth. Oddly, while many dinosaurs, from the ceratopsians to the carnosaurs, produced their largest genus at the very end of the Cretaceous—just before the great extinction sixty-five million years ago—the sauropods didn't. The heyday of these enormous vegetarians came tens of millions of years earlier, during the Jurassic. Apparently common in what is now Texas (and named after the Alamo), *Alamosaurus* roamed as far north as Montana.

Acanthopolis

("Prickly scales"). An ankylosaur, it wore armor that would have made a medieval knight proud. (Actually, you could say that it was a combination of the knight and dragon in a single package.) *Acanthopolis* was 18 feet (5.5 meters) long, and boasted bony plates on its skin and spikes on its neck and back. Like all ankylosaurs, it probably didn't move very fast— but it didn't have to. It lived in England during the Cretaceous.

Allosaurus, Stegosaurus (here shown with two rows of plates), and Diplodocus probably never stood so close together by choice. But they did share the same tropical environment in the western United States during the Late Jurassic.

Albertosaurus

("Alberta lizard"). In its northernmost haunts, *Alamosaurus* might have been hunted by this mid-sized carnosaur, which also roamed the Late Cretaceous grasslands of what is now Alberta, Canada (hence its name—although dozens of different dinosaurs could have been named after this remarkably fossil-rich province). Like its larger cousin, *Tyrannosaurus*, it had small, weak arms, but powerful jaws and legs.

Algoasaurus

("Algo lizard"). This little-known South African sauropod, which resembled the *Brontosaurus*, lived in the Early Cretaceous. The bones of this dinosaur, unearthed at the turn of the century, were among the first ever found in Africa. This exciting find helped convince scientists to journey to that continent in search of fossils. Within a decade, explorers were uncovering some of the greatest troves of dinosaur bones left on earth.

Allosaurus

("Different lizard"). One of the most famous of all dinosaurs, this meat-eater was also among the most widespread, ranging from North America to Australia and Africa. Its strong arms, sharp claws, and fearsome teeth gave it the look of an efficient hunter—but some scientists think that *Allosaurus* (and other large carnosaurs) may actually have survived by eating carrion.

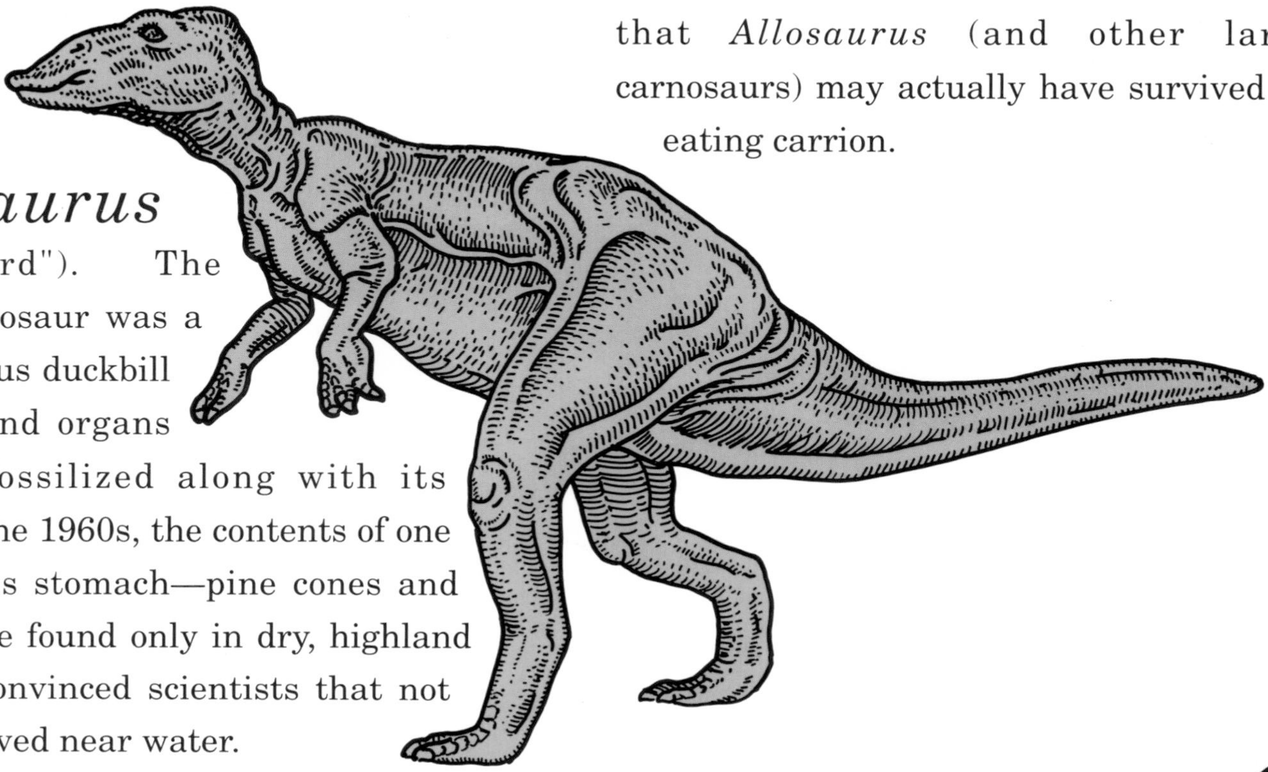

Anatosaurus

("Duck lizard"). The "mummy" dinosaur was a Late Cretaceous duckbill whose skin and organs sometimes fossilized along with its skeleton. In the 1960s, the contents of one such mummy's stomach—pine cones and nuts which are found only in dry, highland areas—first convinced scientists that not all duckbills lived near water.

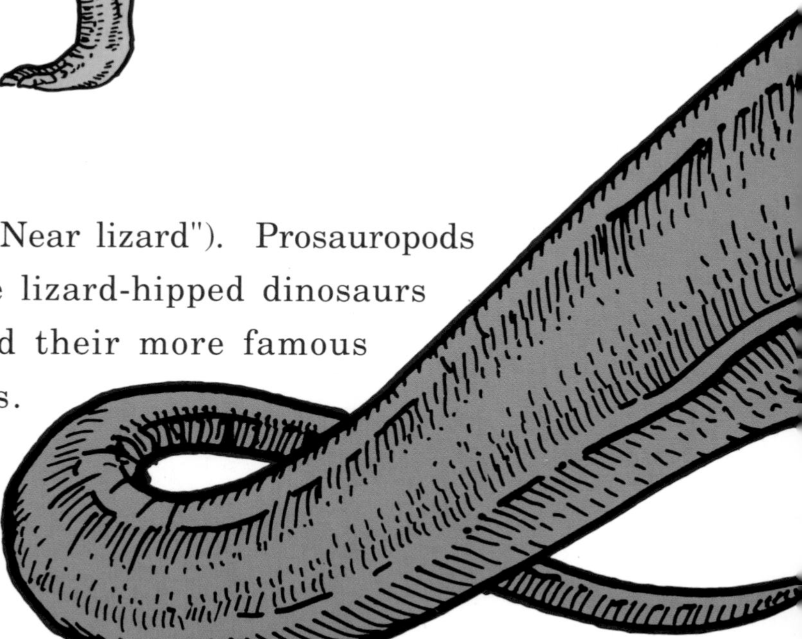

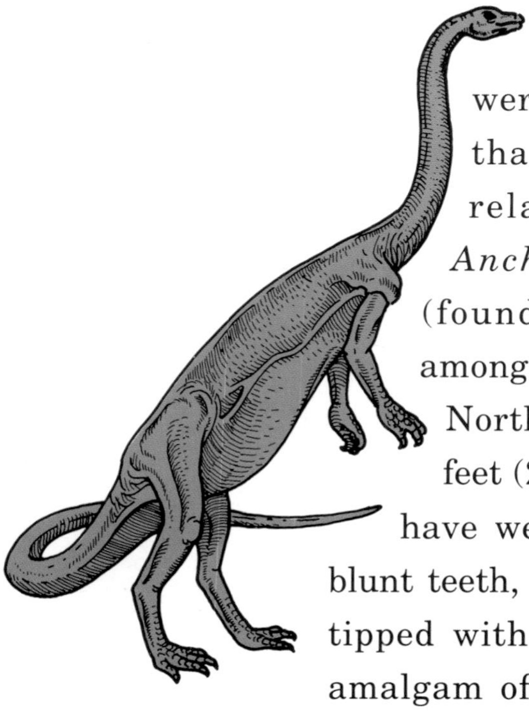

Anchisaurus

("Near lizard"). Prosauropods were comparatively primitive lizard-hipped dinosaurs that often barely resembled their more famous relatives, the sauropods. *Anchisaurus*, whose bones (found in Connecticut) were among the first-ever dug up in North America, was barely 7 feet (2 meters) in length, and may have weighed no more than 50 pounds (23 kilograms). It had blunt teeth, long hind legs, and shorter front legs whose hands were tipped with strong claws on the end of each thumb. This weird amalgam of characteristics make the experts unsure of whether *Anchisaurus* ate plants or meat—or possibly both.

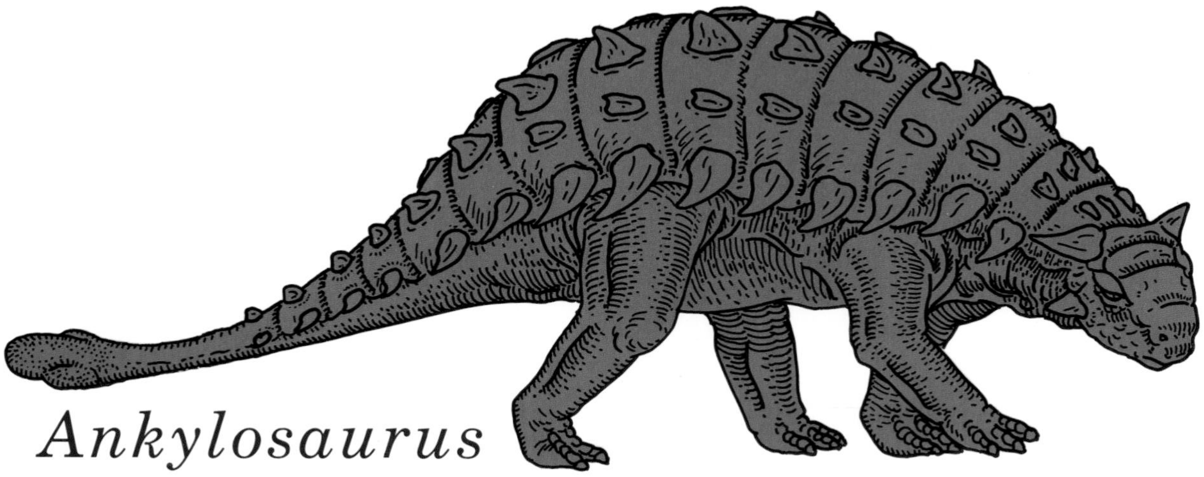

Ankylosaurus

("Stiffened lizard"). At 30 feet (9 meters) or more, this was the largest of all ankylosaurs, and—as usual—one of the last; it died out in the extinction that saw the end of all dinosaurs. Occupying the same haunts as *Tyrannosaurus* and *Triceratops*, *Ankylosaurus* may have been one of the slowest dinosaurs of all time. But its spines, bony armor plates, and clublike tail must have told even the strongest predator that this was one dinosaur not to fool with.

Apatosaurus

("Deceptive lizard"). Think you've never heard of this sauropod? Sure you have—you just know it as *Brontosaurus*, the great "thunder lizard" of so many science fiction books, movies, and museum exhibits. In fact, you'll probably still see this 70-foot (21-meter) giant called by its more familiar name (though the name *Apatosaurus* was given first and used by scientists). By any name it was a massive, small-headed plant-eater that rumbled across the American West in Late Jurassic times.

Archaeopteryx ("Ancient feather"). This is one of the most famous, most beloved, and most controversial of all dinosaurs—and that's saying a lot, given the strong competition. First unearthed in Germany, it initially just looked like a well-preserved small coelurosaur. Then its discoverers looked again—and saw that this was a dinosaur with feathers.

Three-foot *Archaeopteryx*, which lived during the Late Jurassic, boasted many reptile characteristics: sharp teeth, a bony tail, and no large breastbone (which is found in all modern birds, but not in reptiles). Still, it had feathers, leading scientists on an ongoing quest to figure out its place in the dinosaur and bird world.

For many years, most scientists believed that *Archaeopteryx* was a missing link between birdlike dinosaurs, such as *Avimimus* (which may also have had feathers), and actual birds. But in recent years, others have begun to point out that true birds—complete with breastbones, far more powerful wings, and other advanced characteristics—showed up only a few million years after *Archaeopteryx*, far too quickly for the "ancient feather" to be their direct ancestor. Instead, *Archaeopteryx* may have been an evolutionary dead end—the dinosaur that didn't quite make it as a bird.

Despite these uncertainties, scientists agree that *Archaeopteryx* couldn't have been a very good flyer. Instead, it probably used its wings for balance as it pursued its prey, and perhaps for weak gliding.

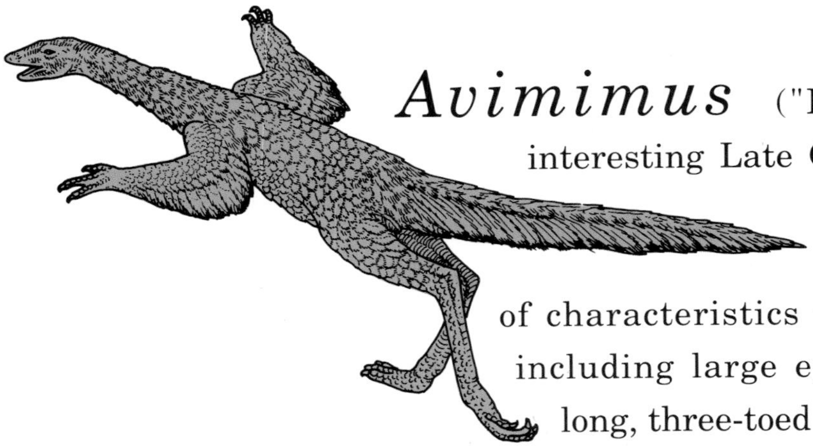

Avimimus ("Bird mimic"). An interesting Late Cretaceous dinosaur, *Avimimus* shared a remarkable number of characteristics with modern birds, including large eyes, a large brain, long, three-toed feet, and lightweight bones. It may even have had feathers on its slender arms. Only 3 to 5 feet (92 centemeters to 1.6 meters) in length, agile *Avimimus* probably ran after the insects and small animals that made up its food.

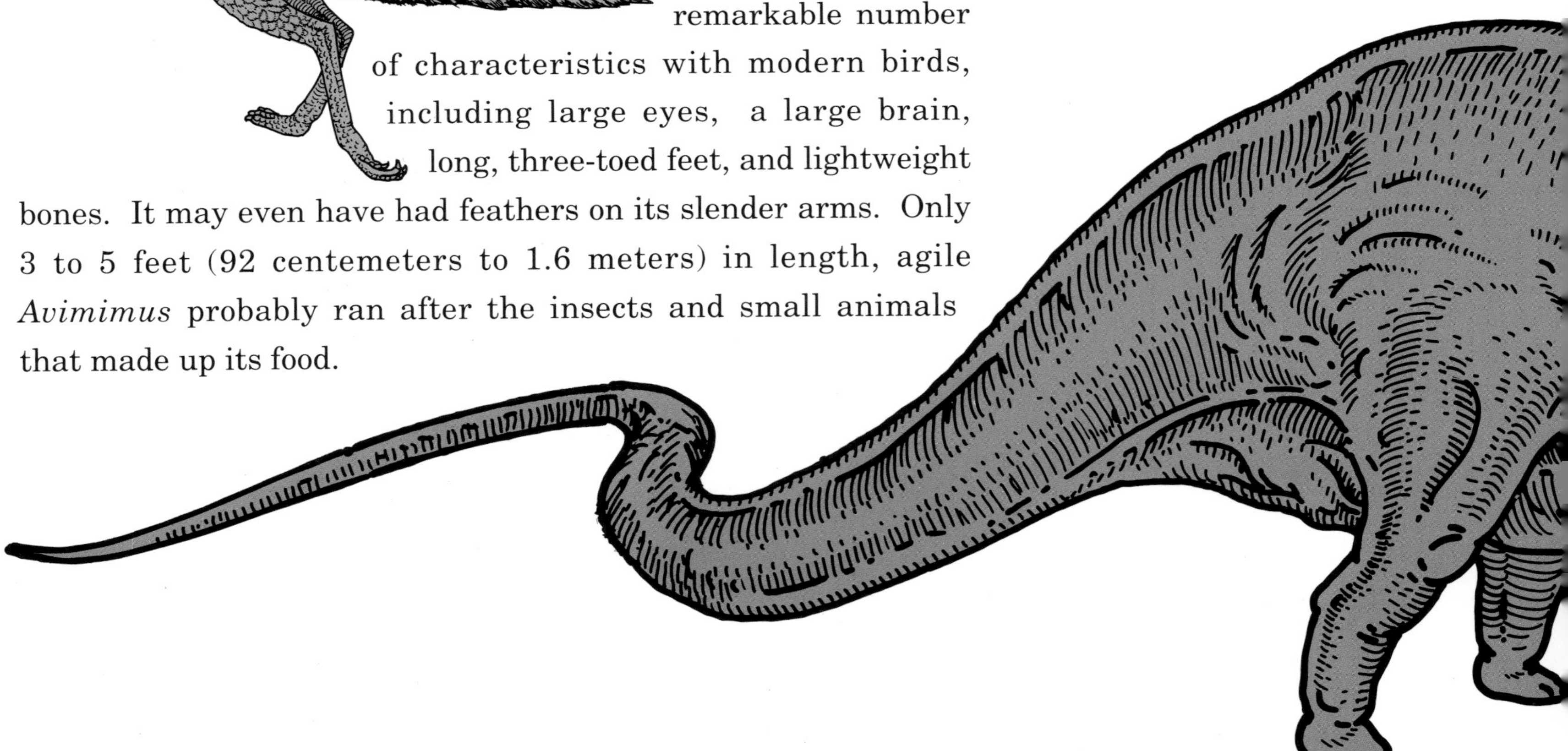

Barapasaurus

("Big-leg lizard"). One of the most ancient of all sauropods, this 60-foot (18-meter) denizen of the Early Jurassic shared many characteristics with the even more ancient prosauropods. It had one feature that puzzles scientists: odd hollow chambers in its backbone. No one knows why, although these chambers must have had some use.

Barosaurus

("Heavy lizard"). The diplodocids, one family of sauropods, were among the longest dinosaurs, yet many were also very lightweight for their size. They must have presented an odd, gawky picture during the Late Jurassic, when they reached their greatest size and abundance. *Barosaurus* was 90 feet (27 meters) long; like the other diplodocids, it had a small, sloping head, weak teeth, and front legs that were far longer than those in back. It lived on the landmass that now constitutes North America and East Africa.

***Daspletosaurus*, a powerful carnosaur, stalked the plains of Alberta, Canada during the Late Cretaceous. Although it may have hunted *Triceratops* and other huge dinosaurs, here it seems to be considering making a meal of *Champsosaurus*, an ancestor of today's alligators.**

Brachiosaurus ("Arm lizard"). Standing as much as 90 feet (27 meters) high and weighing 112 tons (110 metric tons), this may have been the most impressive of all sauropods—as well as one of the most unusual. Its front legs were extremely long (so its back sloped downward), and it also had a long neck and a high forehead, with its nostrils placed above the eyes. Its posture also made *Brachiosaurus* the tallest of all dinosaurs; its tiny head may have hovered a full 40 feet (12 meters) above the ground!

Camarasaurus ("Chambered lizard"). Yet another in a long line of Jurassic sauropods, this one was far more thickly and heavily built than many others. What makes *Camarasaurus* fascinating to scientists is not the creature itself, but a quirk of fate: several skeletons of young *Camarasaurs* have been found. (The delicate, brittle bones of baby dinosaurs rarely fossilize in any recognizable form). *Camarasaurus* babies were remarkably stocky, with big heads, stumpy necks, and short tails.

Camptosaurus

("Bent lizard"). For years, paleontologists have debated whether many ornithopod dinosaurs walked on two legs or four. "Look," one argument went, "they have long hind legs and short front legs, just like any bipedal animal." "Okay," said the other side, "but take a closer look at the skeletal structure. A two-legged dinosaur wouldn't be built that way." So who's right? Examination of the *Camptosaurus* show that both sides were correct: It had the powerful hind legs of a creature accustomed to striding around on two legs. But it also had tiny, hooflike claws on the end of each finger which made it clear that this dinosaur also walked on all fours.

Ceratosaurus

("Horned lizard"). In recent years, scientists have discovered more about the dinosaurs than previous experts could have ever imagined. But certain mysteries seem destined to remain unsolved forever. A case in point: What was the use of the small horn on the end of this Jurassic meat-eater's nose? It couldn't possibly have been used for hunting. Also, *Ceratosaurus*' teeth and claws would have been weapons enough. Perhaps males used the horn in sparring matches to impress the females or to achieve dominance in a herd. But we'll never know for sure.

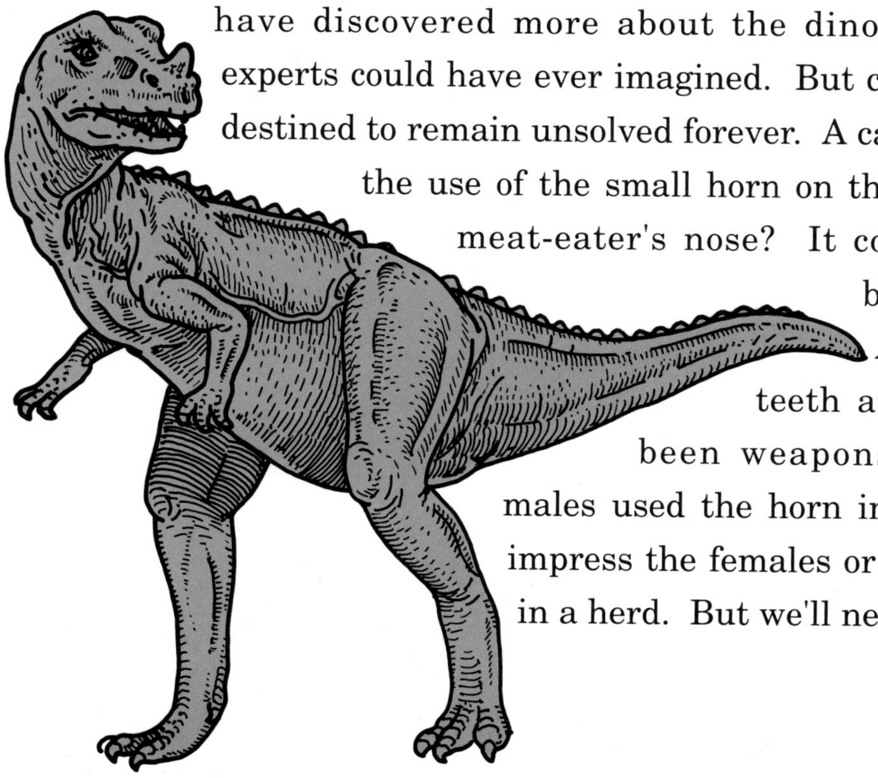

Coelophysis ("Hollow body"). One of the earliest of all known dinosaurs, this slender, 10-foot (3-meter) hunter pursued and caught its prey, probably insects, lizards, and smaller dinosaurs. As is so often the case, we know so much about *Coelophysis* because of an ancient catastrophe. More than 200 million years ago, in what is now New Mexico, a violent sandstorm or other event killed dozens of *Coelophysis* of all sizes, whose fossilized skeletons lay undiscovered until 1947. Some of the larger skeletons had smaller ones inside them, which at first led scientists to think that they were examining unborn babies. Much more likely, the tiny skeletons were just unfortunate juvenile individuals that had recently been eaten by their adult relatives.

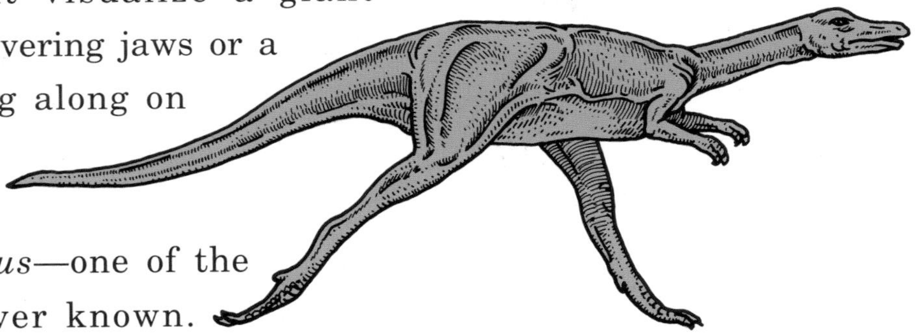

Compsognathus ("Elegant jaw"). Quick, think of a dinosaur. What image comes to mind? You might visualize a giant *Tyrannosaurus* with slavering jaws or a *Brontosaurus* rumbling along on legs like pillars, but you certainly won't think of *Compsognathus*—one of the smallest dinosaurs ever known. Amazingly, this relative of *Coelurus* barely reached a length of 2 feet (61 centimeters), tail and all. It had slender, supple legs, which allowed it to hunt and catch fast-moving lizards and insects.

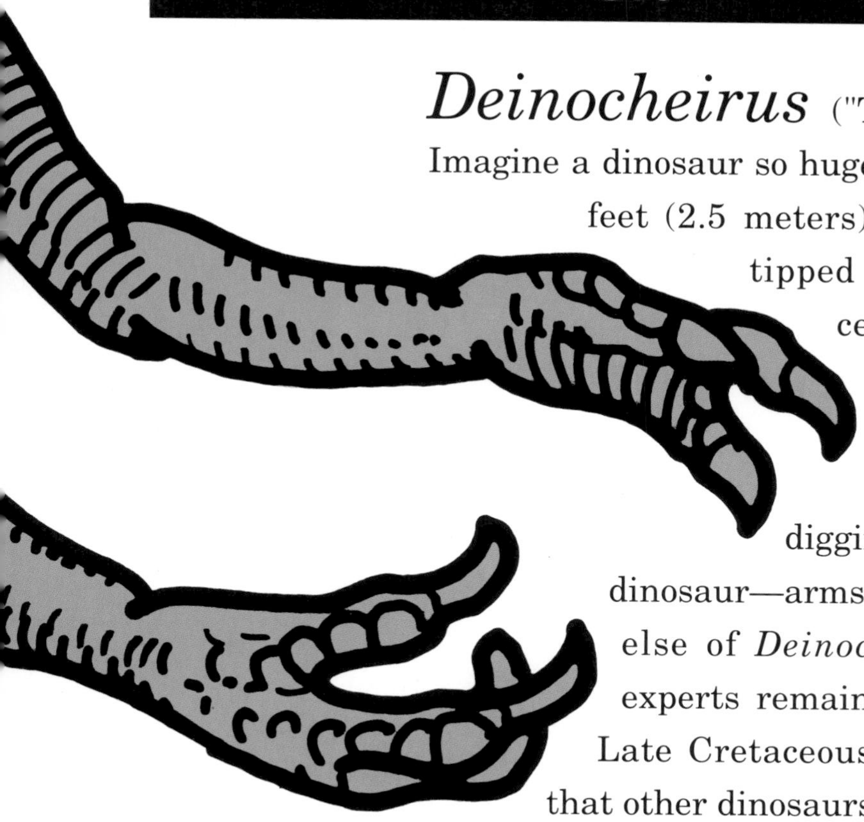

Deinocheirus ("Terrible hand"). Ready for a nightmare? Imagine a dinosaur so huge that each of its arms was more than 8 feet (2.5 meters) long. A creature whose hands were tipped in curved, dagger-sharp 10-inch (26-centimeter) claws, each as lethal as a meat cleaver.

Does this sound unlikely? Well, believe it, because in 1965 scientists digging in Mongolia discovered the arms of a dinosaur—arms that fit this exact description. Nothing else of *Deinocheirus* has ever been found, so the experts remain unsure of exactly what this amazing Late Cretaceous dinosaur looked like. They do know that other dinosaurs must have treated it with respect.

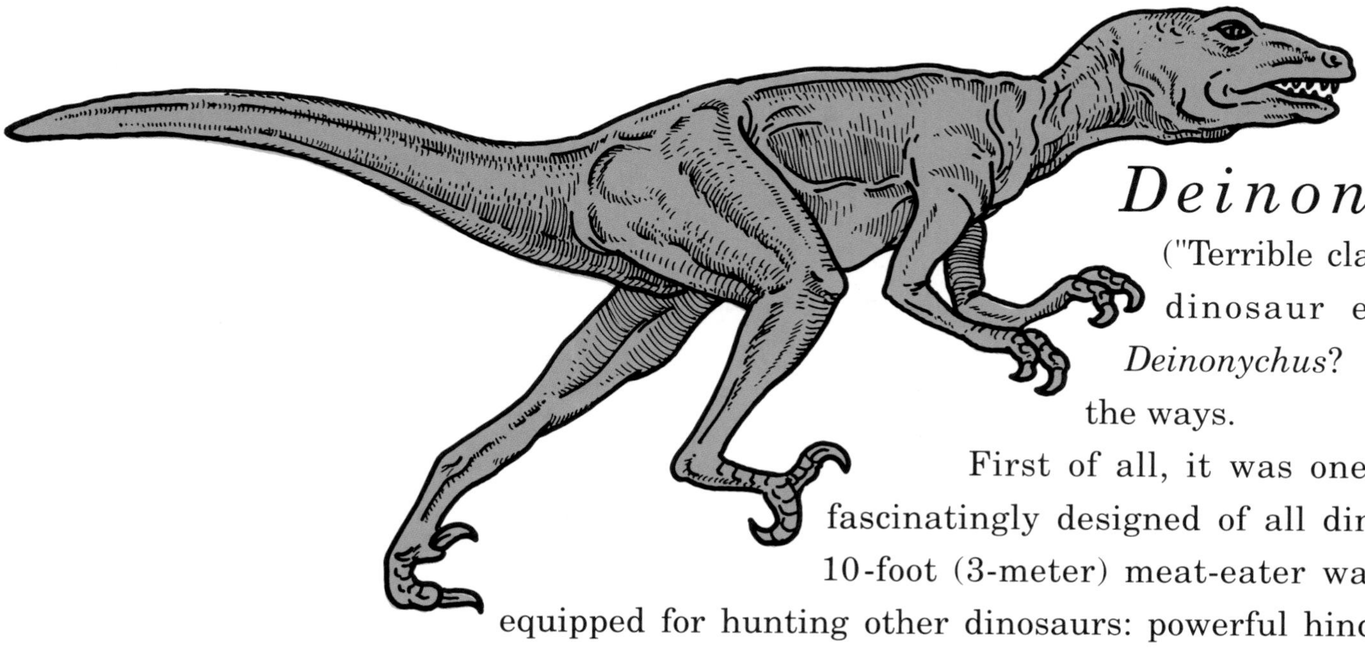

Deinonychus ("Terrible claw"). How do dinosaur experts love *Deinonychus*? Let me count the ways.

First of all, it was one of the most fascinatingly designed of all dinosaurs. This 10-foot (3-meter) meat-eater was fearsomely equipped for hunting other dinosaurs: powerful hind legs, strong arms tipped with sharp claws, a stiffened tail that it used for balance, and—most impressive of all—a special 5-inch (13-centimeter), scythelike claw sprouting from each foot. With these weapons, scientists believe, a group of *Deinonychus* might have chased down even very large dinosaurs, then swung back on one leg and disemboweled the poor victim with their switchblades.

This advanced, active hunting technique gives rise to the second reason that *Deinonychus* is so beloved: No dinosaur has created more controversy, and scientists love controversy. Robert Bakker and others believe that *Deinonychus* must have been warm-blooded, that no cold-blooded dinosaur could possibly have evolved such an energetic hunting style. Many others disagree, and the debate shows no real sign of going away.

Dilophosaurus

("Two-ridged lizard"). An extremely early, primitive carnosaur, this relative of *Megalosaurus* grew to be about 20 feet (6 meters) in length. Like all of its kind, it walked mainly on two legs, and had sharp eyesight and knifelike teeth. It also had one unique attribute: a pair of fragile, bony ridges sitting like a thin crest atop its head. For a long time, scientists refused to believe that this delicate appurtenance came from *Dilophosaurus*, and even now they remain confused as to what its purpose was.

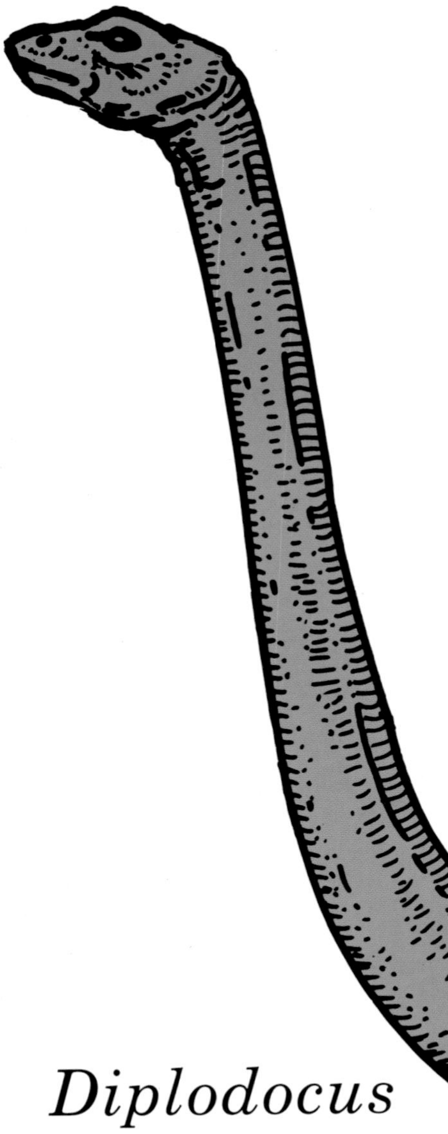

Diplodocus

("Double beam"). If you were a sauropod, you had no choice: You were blessed (or cursed) by certain physical attributes. You had a tiny head, a long neck, a massive body, four legs that resembled Grecian columns, and a seemingly endless, tapering tail. You also had a miniscule brain, and probably spent nearly all your time munching the tender leaves at the tops of trees only you could reach.

If you were *Diplodocus*, a Late Jurassic sauropod found in western North America, you had some of these typical features in abundance. For example, you were one of the longest of the sauropods—up to 90 feet (27 meters) in length—yet you weighed only about 12 tons (11 metric tons), far less than *Apatosaurus*, which weighed in at 30 tons (27 metric tons).

© Brian Regal/Melissa Turk & The Artist Network

Take a good look at *Dilophosaurus's* remarkable crest. What could it have been used for? No one knows for sure, but it may have served as a prominent, colorful display, designed to attract a mate.

Dravidosaurus

("Dravid lizard"). Perhaps the most unusual physical characteristic of this plated dinosaur was the spines on its tail, which featured odd bulges midway along their length. But what really distinguishes *Dravidosaurus* is when it lived: at the very end of the Late Cretaceous, tens of millions of years after *Stegosaurus* and most others. *Dravidosaurus* was the last stegosaur, the one that might have witnessed the end of the dinosaurs' world.

Dromaeosaurus

*("*Swift lizard*").* A pint-sized version of *Deinonychus*, complete with a large brain, strong arms, and a curved claw on each foot. Though only 6 feet (2 meters) long, it probably hunted and killed much bigger dinosaurs, as well as lizards and other smaller prey. Like its larger relative, *Dromaeosaurus* has aroused controversy, with many scientists positive that a sluggish, cold-blooded dinosaur simply could not have managed this fierce little dinosaur's active hunting technique.

Another inhabitant of the marvelously rich Alberta forests and plains, *Dromiceiomimus* may have used its huge eyes to hunt at dawn and dusk, when other dinosaurs were inactive.

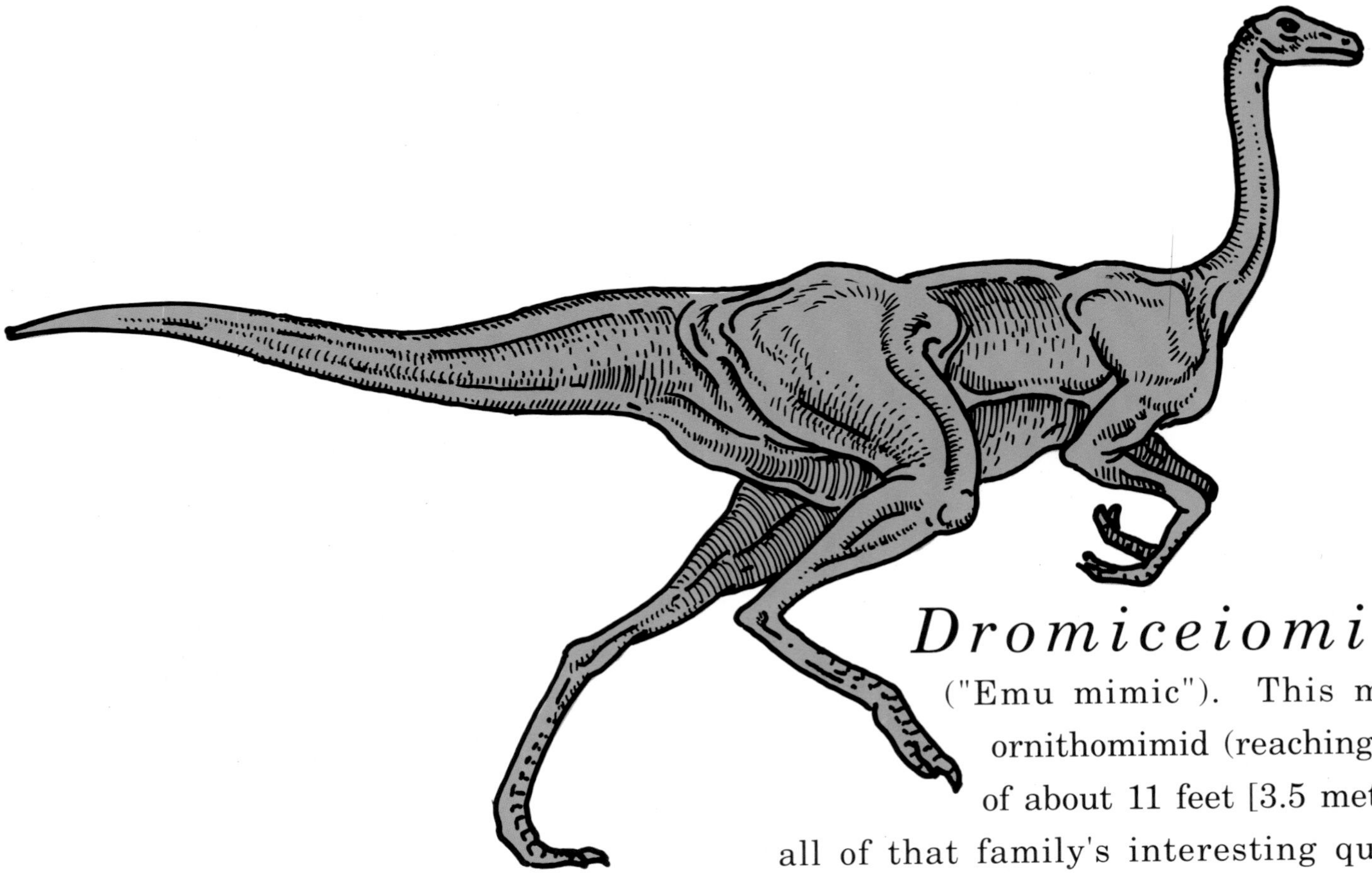

Dromiceiomimus

("Emu mimic"). This mid-sized ornithomimid (reaching a length of about 11 feet [3.5 meters]) had all of that family's interesting quirks and characteristics. *Dromiceiomimus* had a large brain (bigger than an ostrich's), slim but powerful legs, and huge eyes that would have enabled it to remain active at dusk. It lived in the Late Cretaceous in what is now Alberta, Canada—a region that must have been literally crawling with dinosaurs.

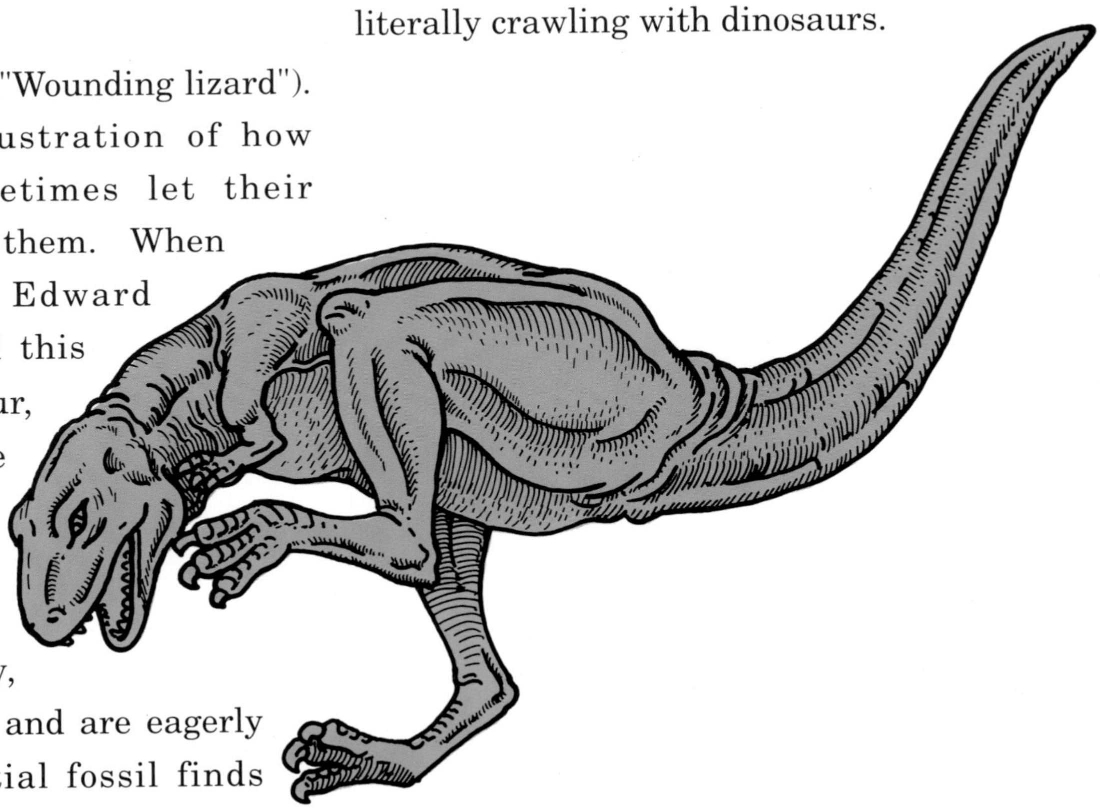

Dryptosaurus

("Wounding lizard"). Here lies a perfect illustration of how dinosaur hunters sometimes let their fantasies run away with them. When famed paleontologist Edward Drinker Cope unearthed this Late Cretaceous carnosaur, he decided (from sparse fossil evidence) that it used its strong hind legs to leap like a kangaroo onto its prey. Today, scientists won't go so far, and are eagerly awaiting more substantial fossil finds before hazarding any guesses as to *Dryptosaurus*' life and habits.

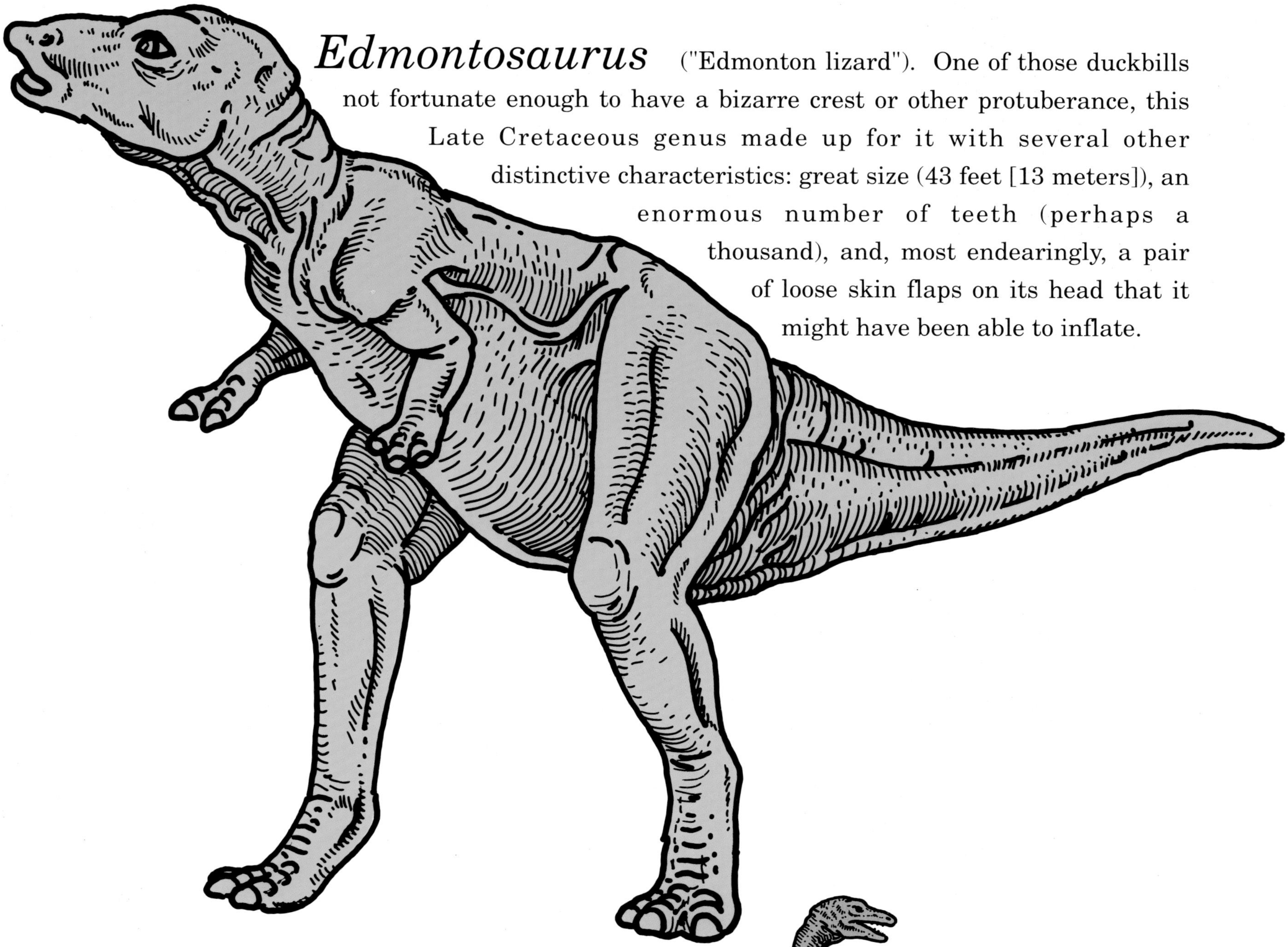

Edmontosaurus ("Edmonton lizard"). One of those duckbills not fortunate enough to have a bizarre crest or other protuberance, this Late Cretaceous genus made up for it with several other distinctive characteristics: great size (43 feet [13 meters]), an enormous number of teeth (perhaps a thousand), and, most endearingly, a pair of loose skin flaps on its head that it might have been able to inflate.

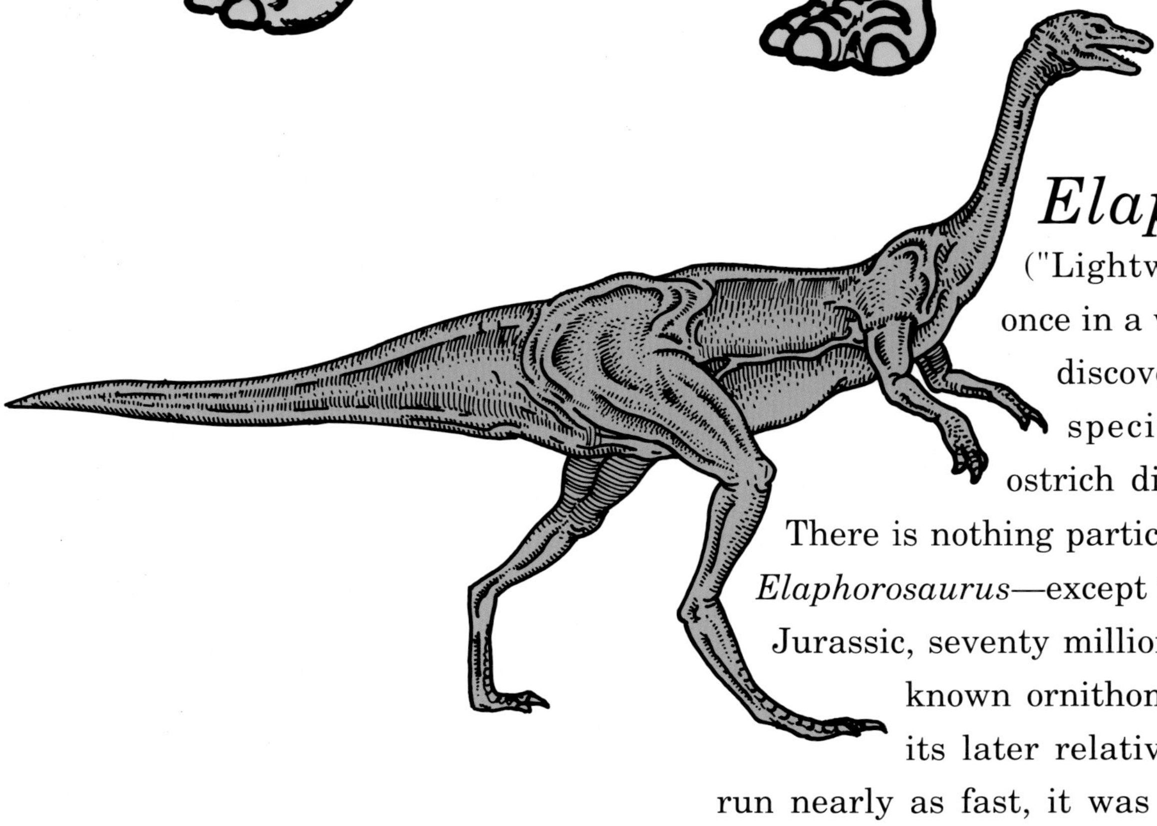

Elaphorosaurus ("Lightweight lizard"). Every once in a while, scientists make a discovery that is particularly special to them, and this ostrich dinosaur is one of them. There is nothing particularly distinctive about *Elaphorosaurus*—except that it lived in the Late Jurassic, seventy million years before all other known ornithomimids. Clumsier than its later relatives, probably unable to run nearly as fast, it was still a fleet-footed and agile predator.

Euoplocephalus

("Well-armored head"). A common North American ankylosaur, *Euoplocephalus* was also a good demonstration of what made those walking tanks so remarkable. Euoplocephalus wore a thick coat of armor that included spines, ridges, bony plates, and probably chunks of bone planted just beneath the skin. But perhaps most impressive was its tail: The last few bones were fused into a solid block tipped with a large club. Even *Tyrannosaurus* would have hesitated before attacking a dinosaur equipped with such powerful defenses.

Fabrosaurus

("Fabre's lizard"). This tiny, primitive ornithischian dinosaur was part of a group that may have developed into all other bird-hipped dinosaurs. Found only in a single region of Southern Africa, it was a lightly built, 3-foot (92-centimeter) plant-eater that ran on its hind legs. Like a herbivorous dinosaur, it must frequently have lost teeth while chewing on tough leaves and seeds. But new teeth would grow in to replace those that fell out.

Gallimimus ("Rooster mimic"). At 13 feet (4 meters), this dinosaur was one of the biggest of all ornithomimids, those birdlike dinosaurs that reached their greatest variety in the Late Cretaceous. With their long, slender legs, skinny necks, and light-boned heads equipped with toothless beaks, *Gallimimus* and the other bird mimics really did resemble such familiar birds as ostriches. They may also have behaved very similarly, striding warily across the plains and scanning the horizon with a sharp eye out for approaching predators.

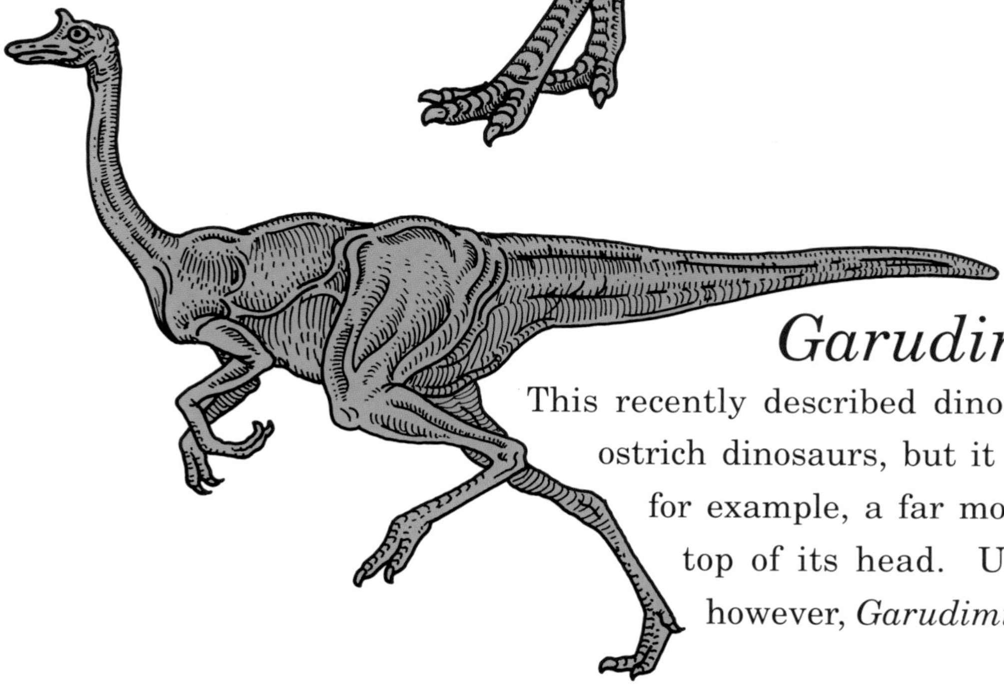

Garudimimus ("Garuda mimic"). This recently described dinosaur was clearly related to the ostrich dinosaurs, but it differed in many ways. It had, for example, a far more rounded beak and a crest on top of its head. Unlike those other bird mimics, however, *Garudimimus* had very large eyes.

Hadrosaurus ("Large lizard"). The *Hadrosaurus* is the namesake for the hadrosaurs, that huge group of duck-billed dinosaurs, abundant in Late Cretaceous times. All were ornithopods that apparently walked easily either on their hind legs or on all fours. They had broad skulls and powerful jaws designed to grind tough vegetation, and many boasted mysterious but wonderfully varied crests. *Hadrosaurus*, unearthed in Alberta, Canada in 1858, was one of the first dinosaurs to be discovered in North America.

Herrerasaurus

("Herrera lizard"). This early, rather primitive lizard-hipped dinosaur was clearly a formidable predator. One of the few dinosaurs whose fossils have been found in South America, this Late Triassic hunter grew to about 10 feet (3 meters), yet weighed only about 200 pounds (75 kilograms). It boasted sharp, curving teeth, long, powerful arms, and individual bones that resembled both those of prosauropods and those of theropods. No one knows yet exactly who *Herrerasaurus*' closest relatives were.

Heterodontosaurus

("Different-toothed lizard"). This was one of the earliest—and most unusual—ornithopods. Roaming Late Triassic or Early Jurassic South Africa, this 4-foot (1.2-meter) dinosaur had three different types of teeth: sharp incisors in front, large molars in the cheek, and pairs of odd, curving tusks growing beside the incisors. No one knows what these tusks may have been used for—or even exactly what *Heterodontosaurus* ate with its strange teeth.

With their large size and ponderous bulk, *Iguanodons* may have sought safety in small herds or family groups. Even so, they likely were frequent prey of local meat-eaters.

Homalocephale ("Even head"). A mid-sized pachycephalosaur, or bonehead dinosaur, found in Mongolia—that hotbed of odd and fascinating fossils. It featured a particularly flat, rough skull, covered—as in many boneheads—with bumps and knobs of bone. But the most interesting discovery about *Homalocephale* has nothing to do with its head, and everything to do with its hips: Some scientists believe that the shape of this dinosaur's hip bones indicates that it didn't lay eggs, but gave birth to live young. By the way, this isn't so astounding. Today, several snake species, including the common North American garter snake, hold the eggs internally until they are ready to hatch, and then give birth to active young, which are immediately ready to strike off on their own. This is very different from the live births seen in warm-blooded birds and mammals, in which the babies are helpless and must be taken care of for days to years.

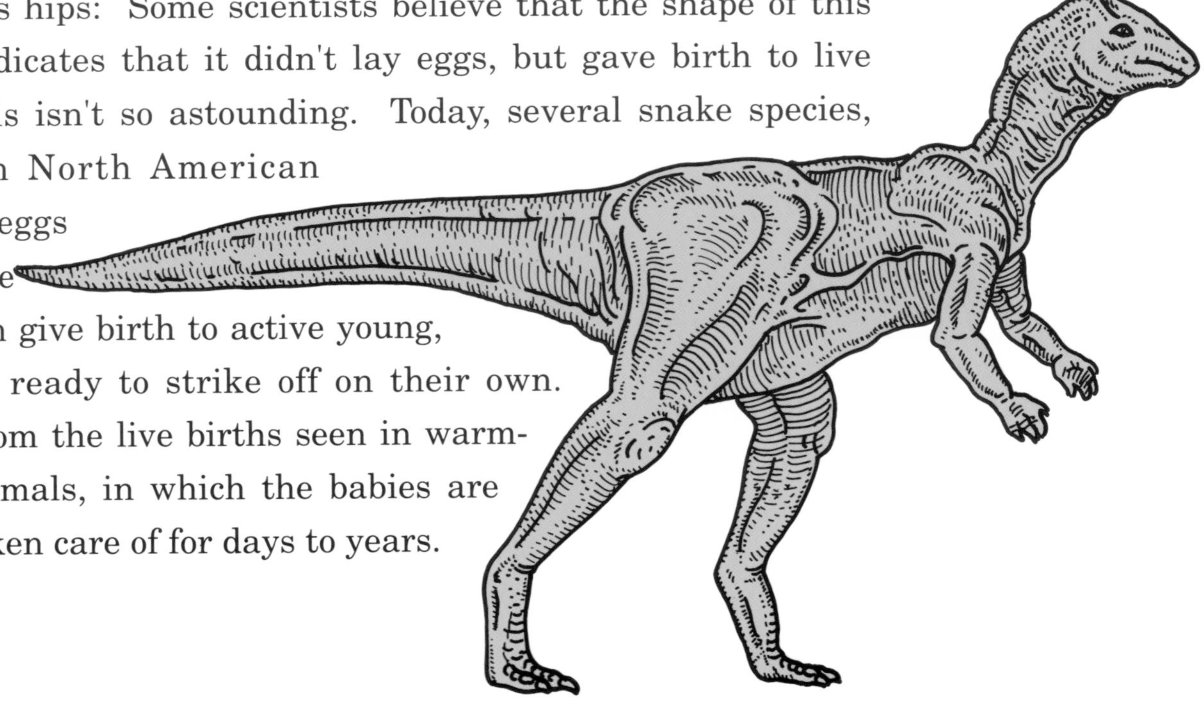

No one knows if *Hypacrosaurus* was really camouflage-green. But there is little doubt that the dinosaurs were far more colorful than early artists (and scientists) thought. This duckbill's leafy environment may well have encouraged the development of green skin.

Hypacrosaurus ("High-ridged lizard"). No dinosaurs were odder looking or more ungainly than the duckbills, with their thick legs, spatula-like mouths, and peculiar crests. *Hypacrosaurus* was one of the largest, about 30 feet (9 meters) in length; its crest formed a high bump atop its skull, leading to a sharp spike that pointed down its back. Even today, scientists argue over the possible purposes of *Hypacrosaurus*' (and other duckbills') crests.

Hypselosaurus

("High lizard"). While the heyday of the sauropods was the Jurassic period (which saw such familiar examples as *Apatosaurus*, *Diplodocus*, and *Brachiosaurus*), many of the great beasts did survive through the Cretaceous. This mid-sized sauropod—about 40 feet (12 meters) long—was a typical example.

Less typical, however, was the discovery of large numbers of eggs found near the bones of *Hypselosaurus* in France. The eggs, the only ones ever identified as having been laid by a sauropod, were about 12 inches (35 centemeters) long—big for dinosaur eggs, but very small for the size of the parent. The eggs were thick-shelled and bumpy.

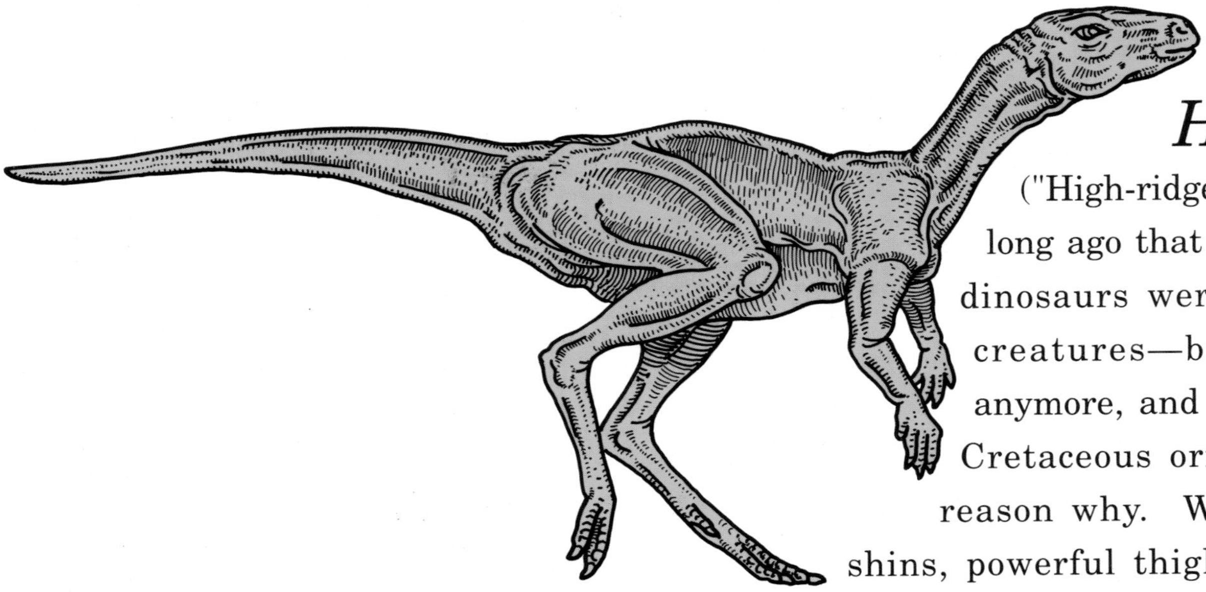

Hypsilophodon

("High-ridged Tooth"). It wasn't very long ago that scientists thought that all dinosaurs were plodding, slow-moving creatures—but they don't think so anymore, and speedsters like this Early Cretaceous ornithopod are part of the reason why. With its supple feet, long shins, powerful thighs, and stiffened tail for balance, *Hypsilophodon* was clearly a sprinter, much like an antelope today. It must have nipped vegetation with its bony beak and chewed with its ridged cheek teeth which were perfectly adapted for pulverizing even the toughest leaves and branches.

Iguanodon ("Iguana tooth").

This thickset Early Cretaceous ornithopod was an abundant ancestor of the widespread duckbills that dominated the Late Cretaceous. Thirty feet (9 meters) long, with a massive head and heavy tail, it was not the most graceful of dinosaurs. Perhaps its most unusual feature was a sharp spike replacing the thumb on each hand—a spike that might have been used as a weapon.

Iguanodon was also one of the earliest dinosaurs to be discovered and identified as a huge, extinct reptile. Gideon and Mary Ann Mantell discovered fossils of this genus in England in 1822. One of the most entertaining sidelights of *Iguanodon*'s recent history is an the early reconstruction of this dinosaur, which showed it as a lumbering, bulky lizard with a tiny horn on its nose. (The horn, of course, was *Iguanodon*'s thumb spike, but only one had turned up when the reconstruction was made.)

Ingenia ("Genius").

Yet another recently discovered oddball Mongolian dinosaur, further proof that this Chinese desert must still contain untold fascinating finds. *Ingenia*, related to the ostrich dinosaurs, was a 6-foot (1.8-meter) meat-eater with powerful hind legs, short, thick fingers, and a toothless jaw ending in a powerful beak. It probably ate eggs, although it might also have hunted or scavenged meat or bones.

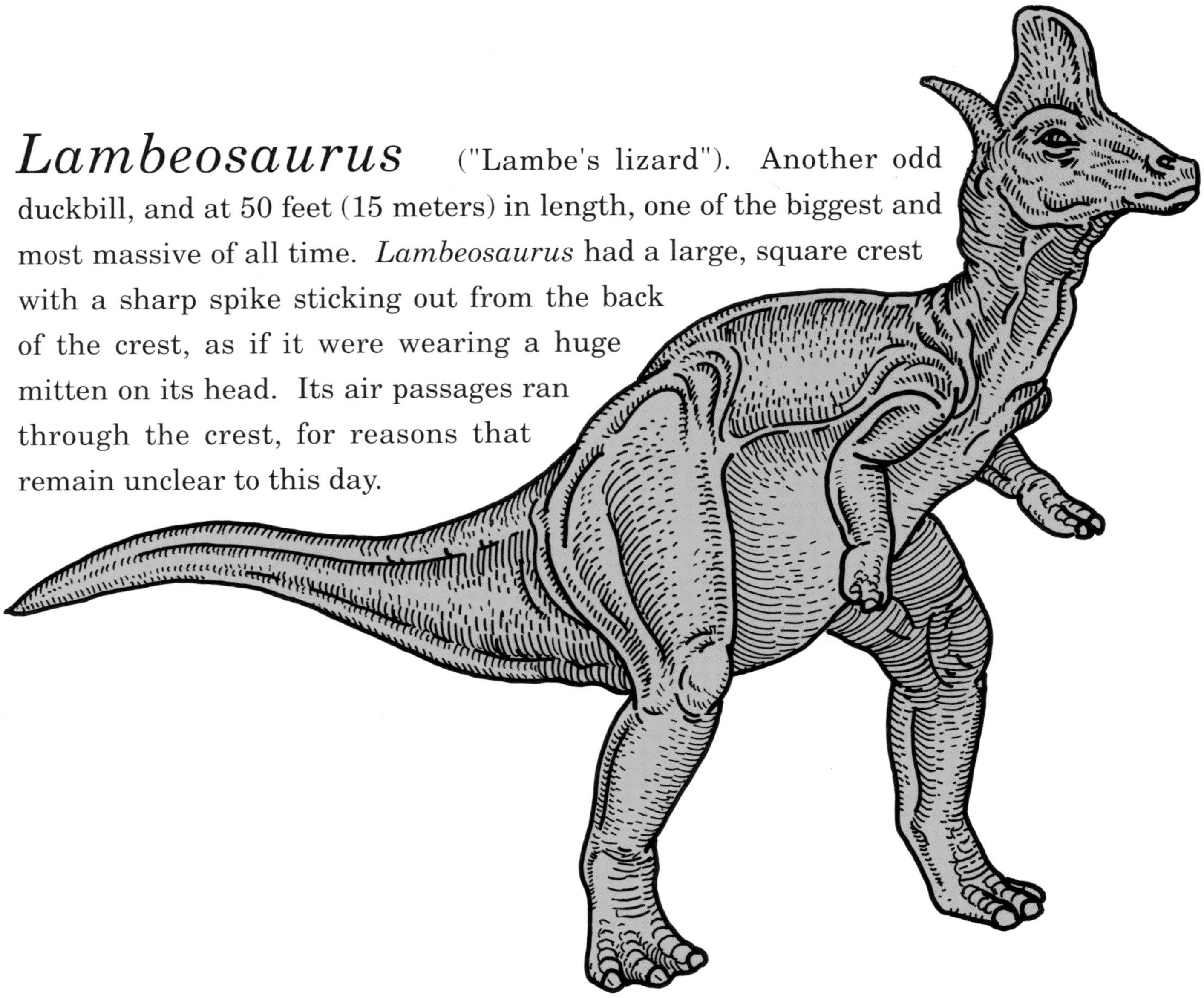

Lambeosaurus ("Lambe's lizard"). Another odd duckbill, and at 50 feet (15 meters) in length, one of the biggest and most massive of all time. *Lambeosaurus* had a large, square crest with a sharp spike sticking out from the back of the crest, as if it were wearing a huge mitten on its head. Its air passages ran through the crest, for reasons that remain unclear to this day.

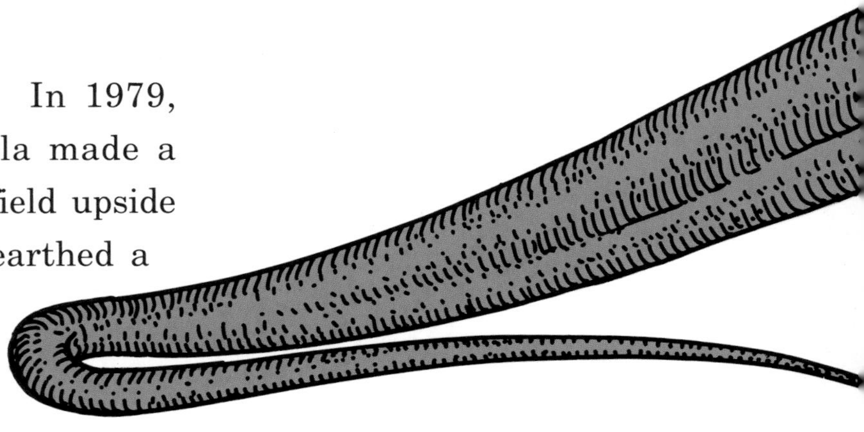

Maiasaura ("Good-mother lizard"). In 1979, paleontologists John Horner and Robert Makela made a dinosaur discovery that turned the paleontology field upside down. In a barren region of Montana, they unearthed a slew of skeletons of a previously unknown duckbill, a 30-foot (9-meter) creature that physically wasn't very different from many other species. What was different—and exciting—was the discovery of fossilized mud nests, enough of them to prove for the first time that at least one type of dinosaur lived and bred in colonies.

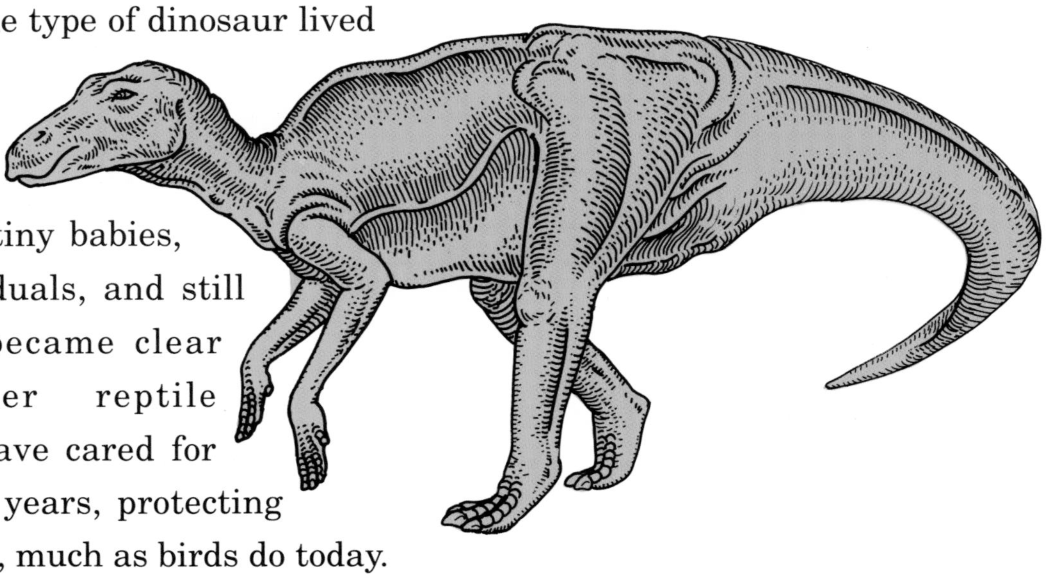

But what astounded the two scientists was that the skeletons included some of tiny babies, others of half-grown individuals, and still others of adults. So it became clear that—unlike any other reptile known—*Maiasaura* must have cared for its babies for months, even years, protecting them and bringing them food, much as birds do today.

Mamenchisaurus ("Mamenchin lizard"). More or less, every sauropod looked alike. But only more or less. This remarkable Late Jurassic individual, whose bones were found in southern China, stands out for one simple feature: its neck. The beast itself was about 70 feet (21 meters) long—and a full half the length was made up by its neck. This 35-foot (11-meter) extravaganza contained nineteen vertebrae, more than any other dinosaur. Rods of bone running alongside the vertebrae provided needed strength and stability to a neck that must have been a remarkable sight.

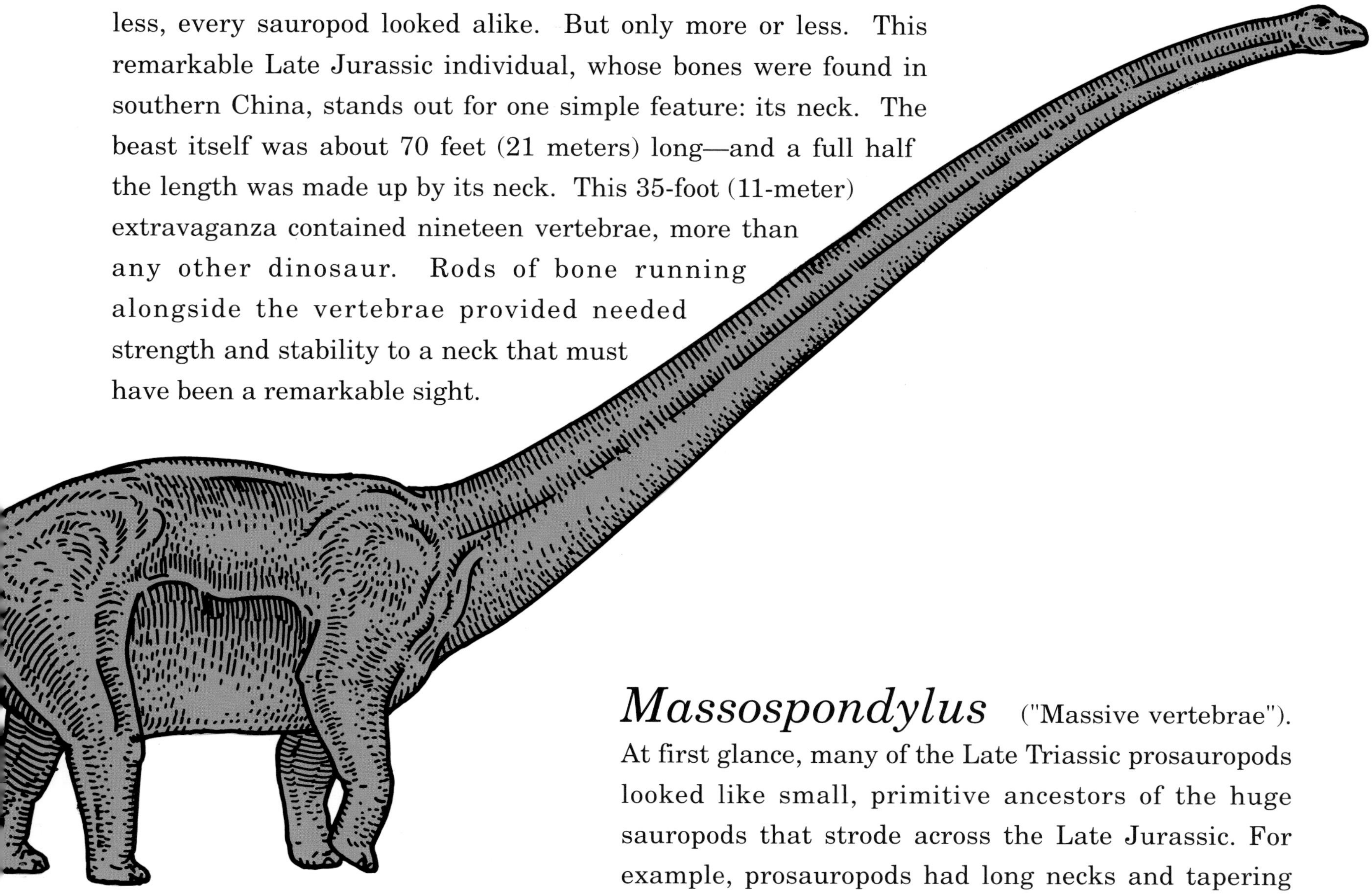

Massospondylus ("Massive vertebrae"). At first glance, many of the Late Triassic prosauropods looked like small, primitive ancestors of the huge sauropods that strode across the Late Jurassic. For example, prosauropods had long necks and tapering tails, much like their more famous relatives.

But, as this 13-foot (4-meter) individual shows, prosauropods and sauropods had some distinctive differences. *Massospondylus* had very strong and flexible hind legs, and its front legs ended in grasping hands, including a thumb equipped with a curving claw. These features make it likely that *Massospondylus*, like other prosauropods but unlike the sauropods, may have spent some time walking on its hind legs.

© Doug Henderson

Maiasaurs **may have been one of the most common dinosaurs along the eastern front of the Rocky Mountains during the Cretaceous. We know that because so many thousands of them were killed by this enormous ashfall 100 million years ago.**

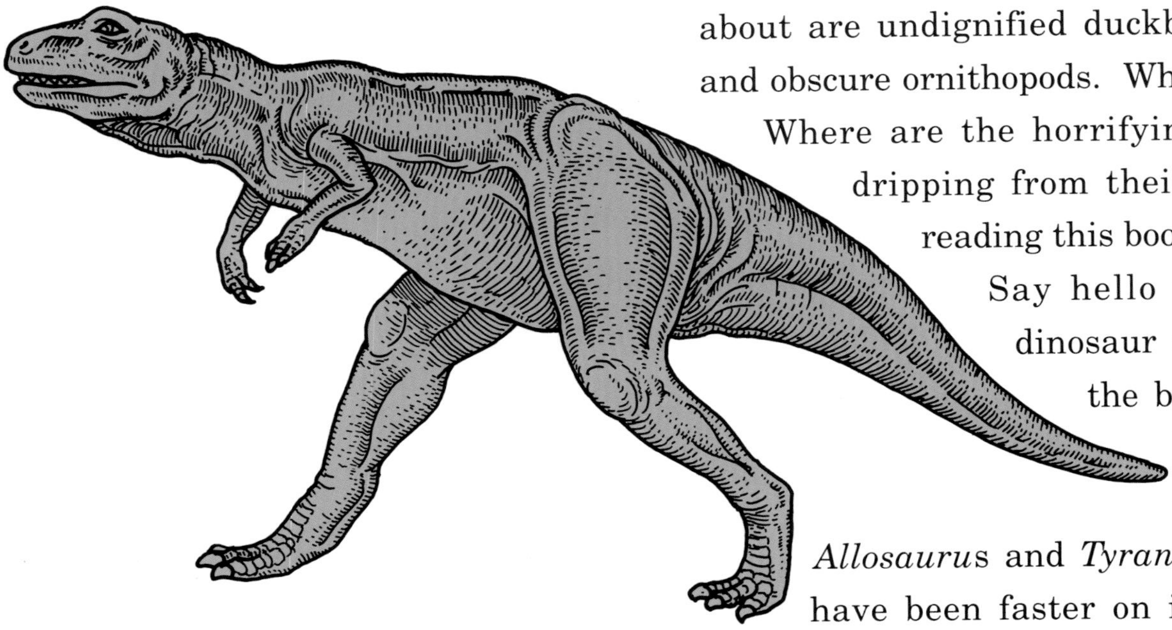

Megalosaurus

("Huge lizard"). All right, all right, I know what you're thinking: "All he's telling us about are undignified duckbills, plodding prosauropods, and obscure ornithopods. Where are all the fun dinosaurs? Where are the horrifying predators with the blood dripping from their fangs? That's what we're reading this book for."

Say hello to *Megalosaurus*, the first dinosaur ever to be named and one of the best-designed predators in the history of the earth. Smaller than its more familiar cousins *Allosaurus* and *Tyrannosaurus*, *Megalosaurus* may have been faster on its feet and more agile than those great meat-eaters. With strong, curving claws on its feet and hands, and long, serrated teeth, it would have been a threat to any dinosaur that crossed its path.

Melanorosaurus

("Black-mountain lizard," also known as *Euskelosaurus*). Until fairly recently, experts thought that the great sauropods were direct descendants of prosauropods—and this 40-foot (12-meter) plodder was powerful evidence for that theory. Huge, heavy, and possessing four legs good only for walking (unlike other prosauropods, which had arms and hands), Late Triassic *Melanorosaurus* did, in fact, closely resemble the sauropods.

But in paleontology (to paraphrase Yogi Berra), you don't know *nothin'*. Today, many scientists think that prosauropods and sauropods were just different branches on the same family tree, with no direct relationship.

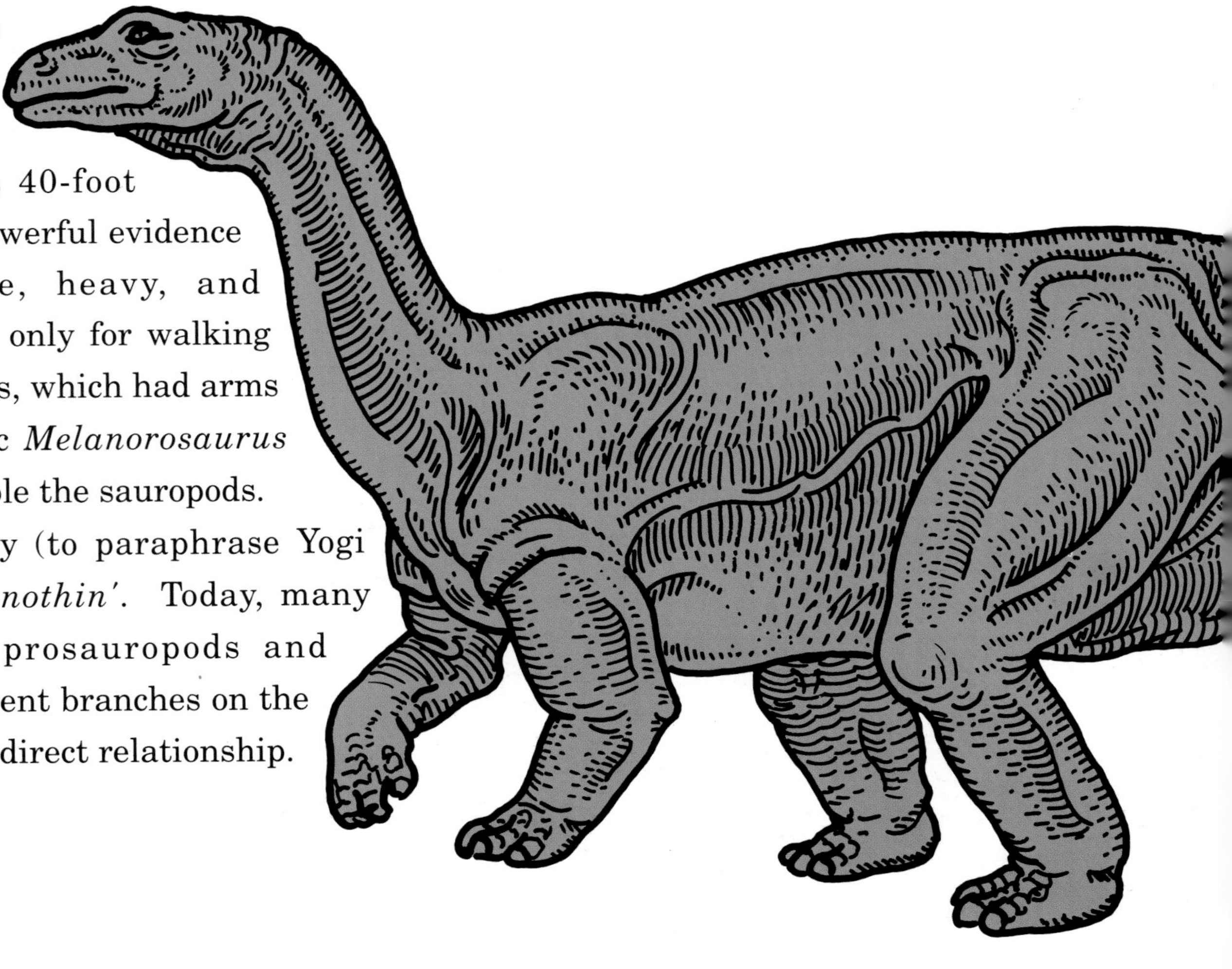

Mussasaurus

("Mouse lizard"). Okay, had your fill of giant dinosaurs? Well, take a look at something completely different: *Mussasaurus*, the world's smallest dinosaur.

Actually, we don't know for sure if this prosauropod was the smallest dinosaur—but we do know that its babies (and probably its eggs) were incredibly tiny. A fossilized egg that scientists think was laid by a *Mussasaurus* measured about an inch (3 centimeters) in length. Almost as amazing, babies found in a nest were no longer than 8 inches (24 centimeters). That's about as big as a robin.

Muttaburrasaurus

("Muttaburra lizard"). As well as having one of the most endearing of all dinosaur names, this Late Cretaceous relative of *Iguanodon* is one of the only dinosaurs ever found in Australia. Experts think that many more dinosaur remains will eventually be found in Australia, once enough scientists brave its harsh deserts in the search for fossils.

Nanotyrannus ("Pygmy tyrant"). One of the things that makes the world of dinosaurs so fascinating and enjoyable to follow is that—despite the fact that the great reptiles have been extinct for sixty-five million years—nothing in paleontology stays the same for very long.

Back in 1942, dinosaur hunters in Montana brought a load of fossils to the Cleveland Museum of Natural History in Ohio. Among these fossils was the skull of what they thought was an *Albertosaurus*, a very common Late Cretaceous carnosaur. The museum already had good examples of *Albertosaurus*, so the skull was labeled and filed away, where it lay untouched for many years.

Then, in 1988, a group of paleontologists headed by Robert Bakker challenged the identification. By examining the skull closely, they found that it actually shared many characteristics with *Tyrannosaurus*, although it weighed only one-tenth as much. Yet the fully fused bones showed that the skull must have belonged to a previously unknown adult dinosaur, and not a baby tyrannosaur.

Nanotyrannus was, scientists think, an exact, although miniaturized, replica of its famous giant cousin. Reaching a length of about 17 feet (5.3 meters), and weighing in at about 1000 pounds (455 kilograms), it was equipped with a large brain, relatively weak arms and hands, and a long, narrow muzzle filled with sharp, curving, serrated teeth. In other words, this pygmy tyrant must have been an agile, powerful hunter.

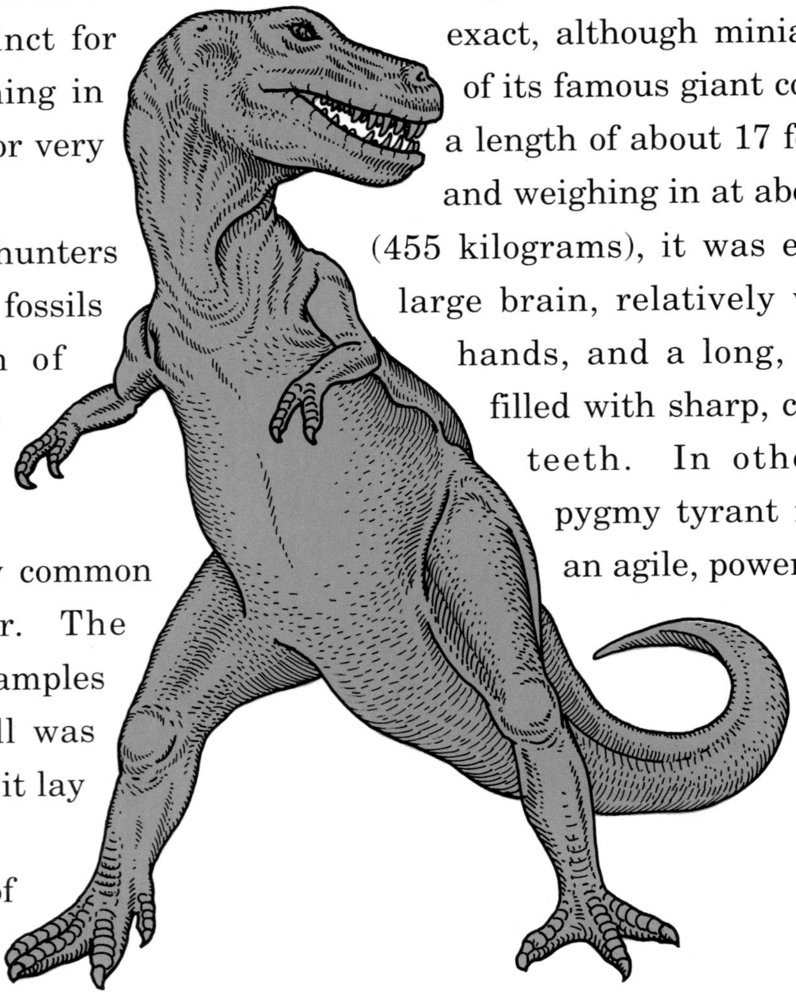

Noasaurus ("Northwest Argentina lizard"). A South American relative of *Deinonychus*, this Late Cretaceous theropod was smaller than its fearsome relative. But, it too, featured a slashing switchblade claw, with which it may have attacked far larger dinosaurs. If, as many scientists believed, coelurosaurs (including *Noasaurus*) often hunted in packs, they may have been the most feared dinosaur predators of all.

Opisthocoelicauda ("Backward hollow tail"). This unusual Late Cretaceous sauropod illustrates what makes paleontology both a rewarding and a frustrating profession. When a nearly complete skeleton of this 40-foot (12-meter) dinosaur was discovered in the Gobi Desert in Mongolia, scientists soon found that it had an odd set of tail bones that may have allowed it to prop itself up on its hind legs. But the fossil record giveth and taketh away: this skeleton was missing a head and neck, and no others have ever been found, so the experts have never been able to study *Opisthocoelicauda* thoroughly enough.

Ornitholestes ("Bird robber"). Another one of those swift, lightweight hunters that don't fit in with the theory that dinosaurs were heavy-footed creatures. No more than 7 feet (2.2 meters) long, with a slender neck, grasping hands, and powerful legs, *Ornitholestes* got its name from its supposed ability to catch birds. More likely, it pursued and grabbed lizards and small mammals.

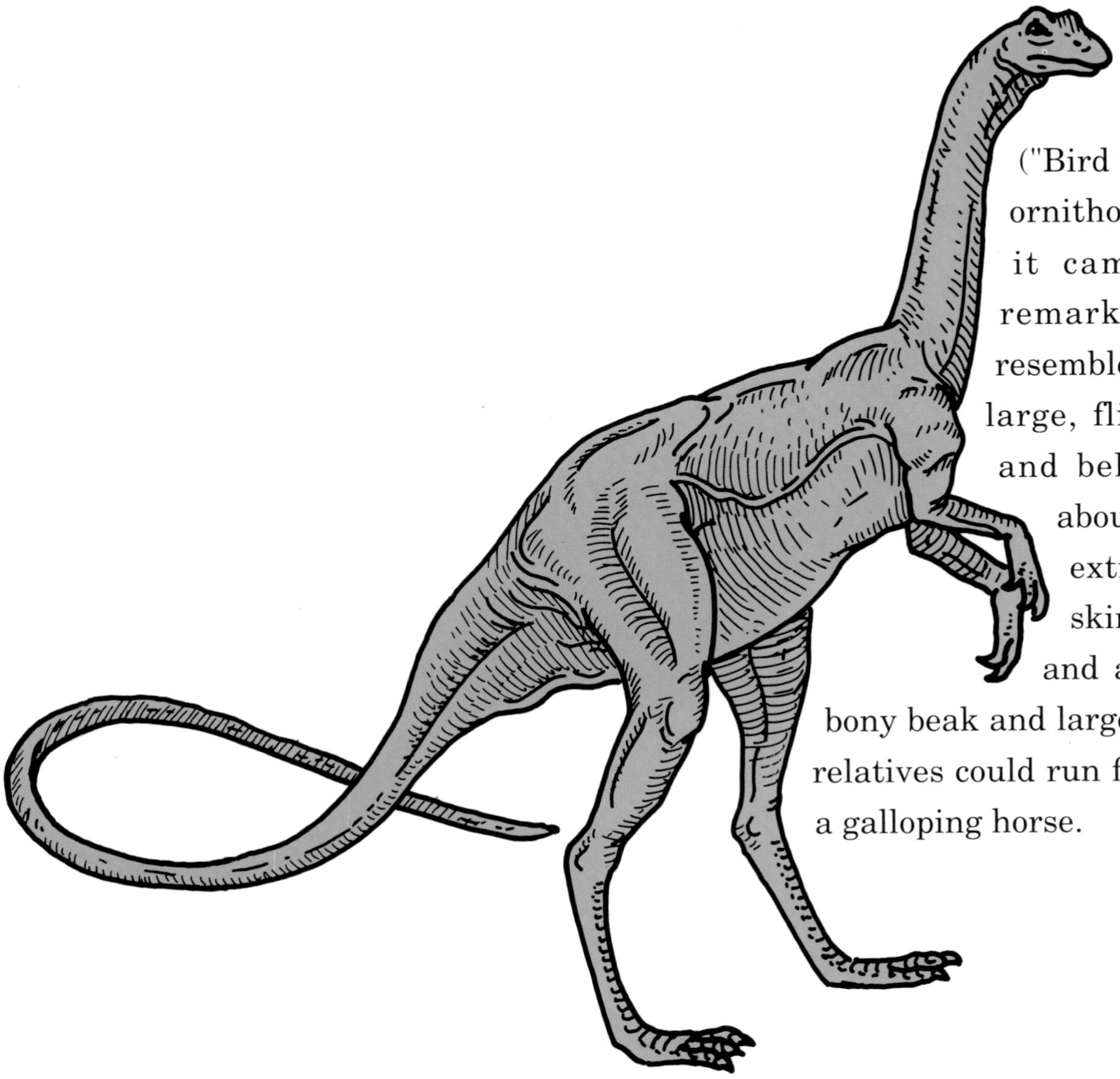

Ornithomimus

("Bird mimic"). The namesake of the ornithomimids or ostrich dinosaurs, it came from a large group of remarkable dinosaurs that closely resembled ostriches, emus, and other large, flightless birds in both shape and behavior. *Ornithomimus* was about 12 feet (4 meters) long, had extremely thin and supple legs, skinny arms, a very slender neck, and a small head equipped with a bony beak and large eyes. *Ornithomimus* and its relatives could run fast—perhaps even faster than a galloping horse.

Orodromeus

("Mountain runner"). One of the latest of the seemingly unending slew of fascinating dinosaur discoveries made by Jack Horner in Montana, this member of the hypsilophodontid family (which also contains *Dryosaurus* and other antelope-like dinosaurs) was itself cause for celebration.

But what made this 1987 find even more exciting was that it came with a clutch of nineteen unhatched eggs, many of which contained fossilized skeletons of the enclosed embryos. Using CT scans (high-powered x-rays), Horner and his coworkers were able to study the embryos closely, and identify them as belonging to a newly created genus and species: *Orodromeus makelai.* It reached a length of about 8 feet (2.5 meters), they believe, and was (like most of its family) among the fastest-moving of all dinosaurs.

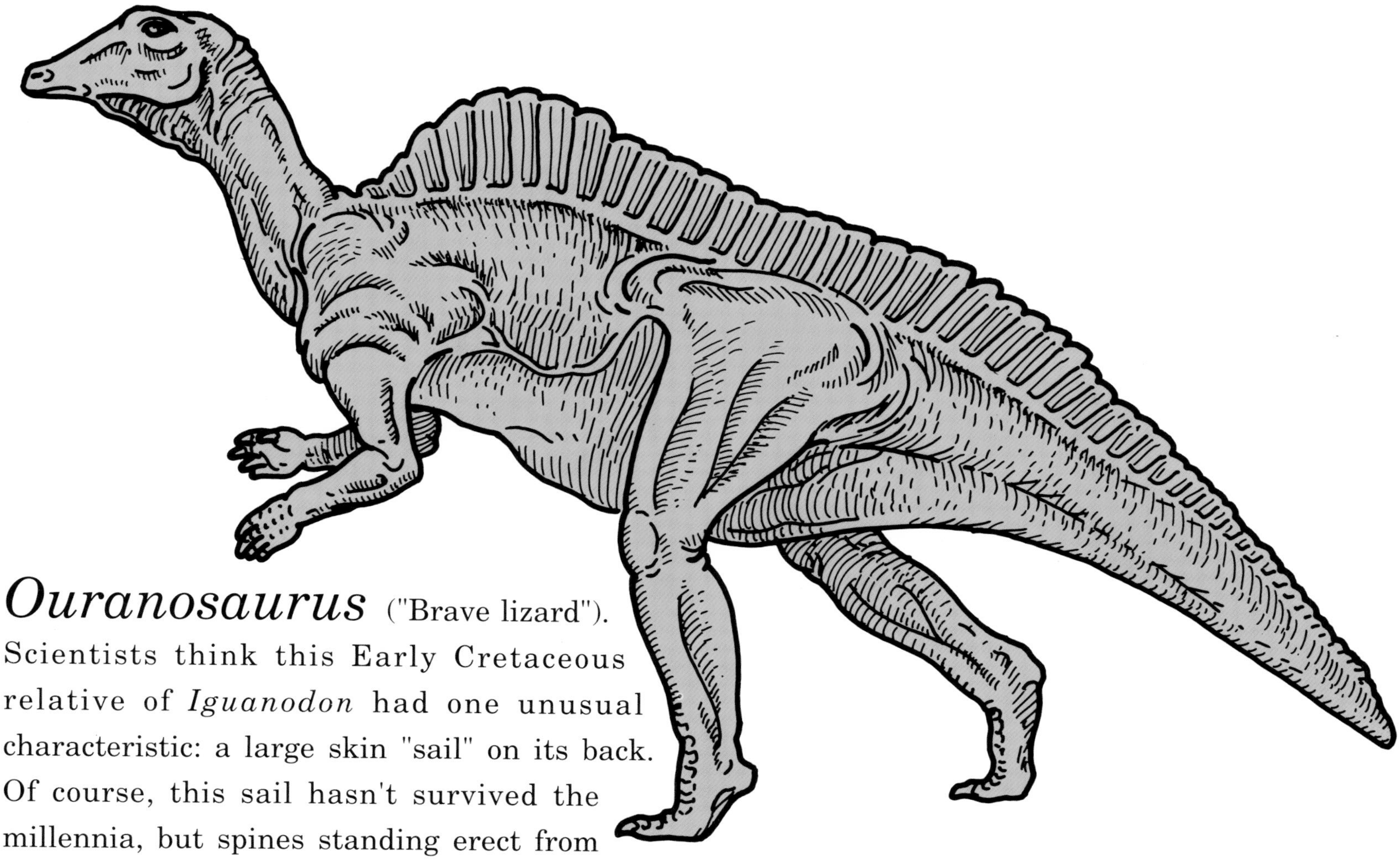

Ouranosaurus ("Brave lizard"). Scientists think this Early Cretaceous relative of *Iguanodon* had one unusual characteristic: a large skin "sail" on its back. Of course, this sail hasn't survived the millennia, but spines standing erect from the dinosaur's backbone almost certainly evolved to support such a flap of skin. The sail might have been used as a "heat exchanger": that is, when the dinosaur was cold, turning the sail to the sun would have enabled it to absorb extra rays. On the other hand, on a hot day, *Ouranosaurus* could have sought shade, then radiated heat more rapidly through the skin flap.

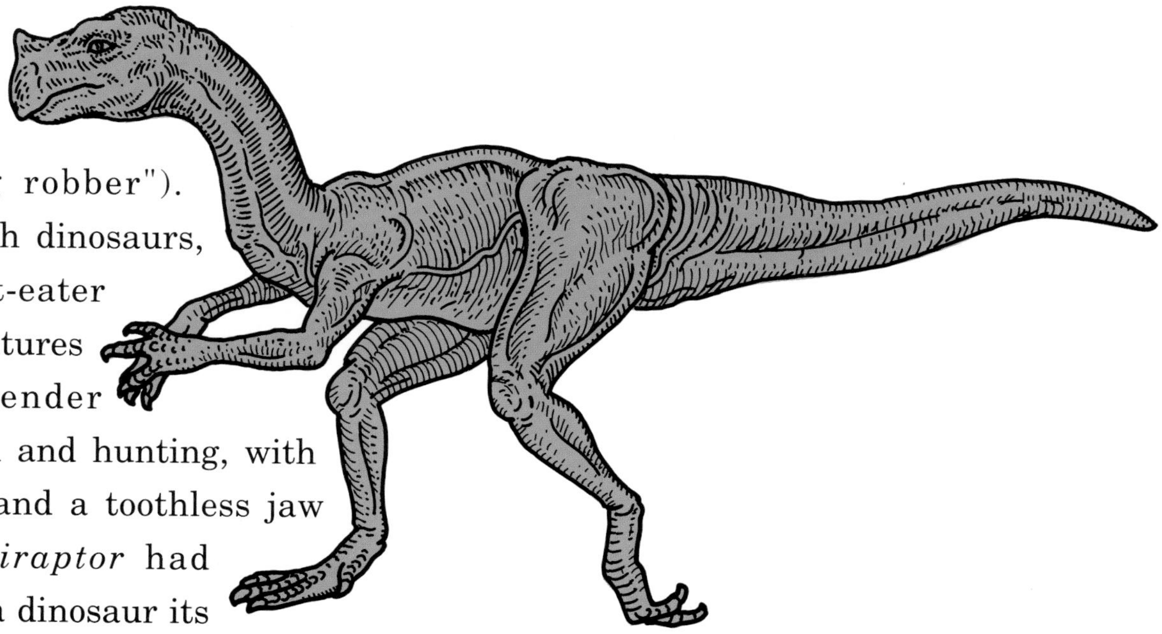

Oviraptor ("Egg robber"). Although related to the ostrich dinosaurs, this 6-foot (1.85-meter) meat-eater boasted several fascinating features of its own. Like those slender reptiles, it was built for speed and hunting, with strong legs, grasping hands, and a toothless jaw ending in a beak. But *Oviraptor* had remarkably powerful jaws for a dinosaur its size; its beak would easily have chewed up bones, as well as the eggs that it probably also ate.

Pachycephalosaurus

("Thick-headed lizard"). For unclear reasons, the Late Cretaceous was the glory period for bizarre dinosaurs—and few were odder than the *Pachycephalosaurs* or bonehead dinosaurs. These two-legged plant-eaters had bodies that resembled the duckbills, but skulls that looked like nothing else on earth. Nearly every bonehead had a massively thick, domed skull; *Pachycephalosaurus*' was 10 inches (25 centimeters) thick!

What was the purpose of such thick skulls? We may never know for sure, but some experts believe that male boneheads might have fought for dominance in the herd by banging their heads together, much as bighorn sheep do today.

Pachycephalosaurus itself was the biggest bonehead, with the thickest skull. It grew to be about 15 feet (5 meters) in length, and lived, like so many other Late Cretaceous dinosaurs, in western North America.

Pachyrhinosaurus

("Thick-nosed lizard"). When is a horned dinosaur not a horned dinosaur? When it's *Pachyrhinosaurus*, a relative of the familiar *Triceratops* that came equipped with no horns at all. Instead, it had a mass of bone between its eyes that couldn't have provided a very effective weapon. Its chief protection must have been its large size (up to 20 feet [6.2 meters]) and thick, tough skin.

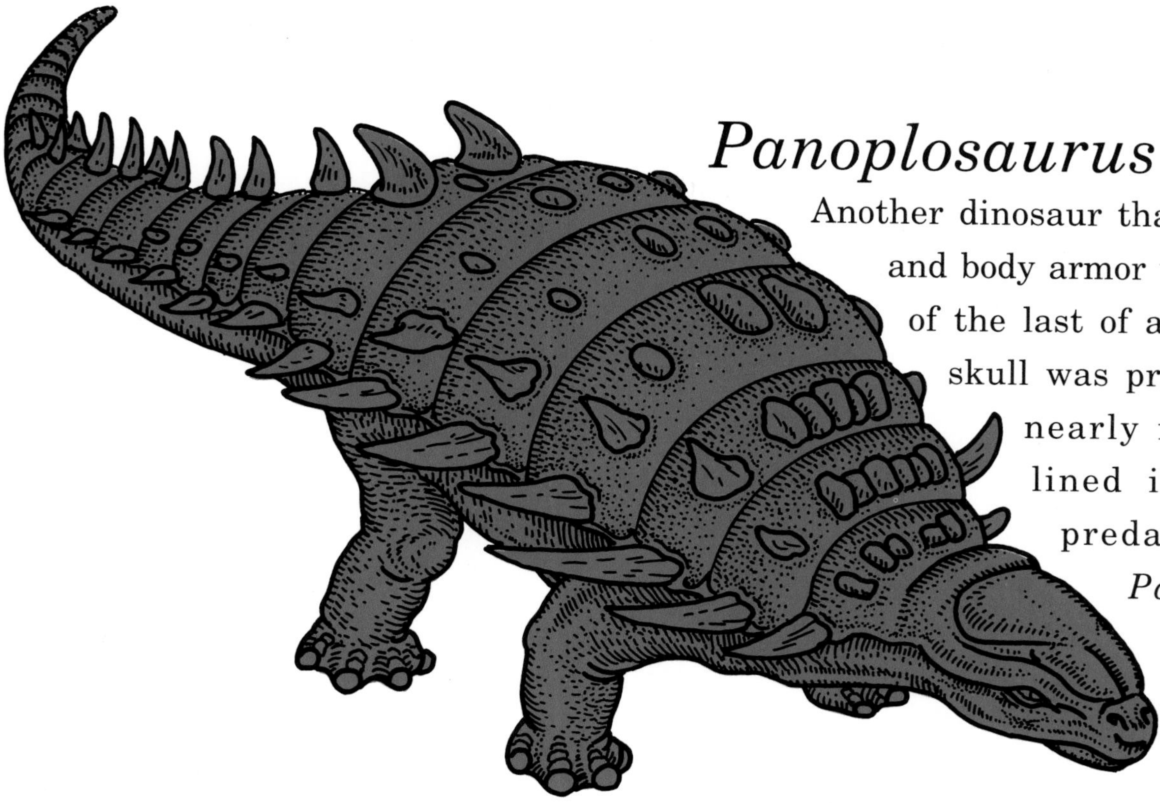

Panoplosaurus

("Fully-armored lizard"). Another dinosaur that must have relied on size and body armor was the *Panoplosaurus*, one of the last of all ankylosaurs. Its arched skull was protected by thick bone, and nearly impregnable bony plates lined its back. For a roving predator, attempting to kill *Panoplosaurus* must have been about as easy as opening a can of tuna without an opener.

Parasaurolophus

("Like *Saurolophus*"). Among the duckbills—a group of dinosaurs well-known for their bizarre appearance—*Parasaurolophus* somehow managed to be even weirder than most of the rest. Its body was a typical duckbill's: thickset, with strong hind legs, fleshy arms, and a flat, ducklike mouth. But atop its skull stood an amazing hollow horn up to 6 feet (1.8 meters) long. And that's not all: The dinosaur's breathing passages ran from its nostrils up one side of the horn, down the other, and out into the creature's mouth.

Why? Good question—one that scientists still aren't sure they have the answer to. But some think that the hollow horn (found, in various shapes, in many duckbills) might have functioned as an echo chamber, allowing the dinosaur to make loud honking sounds. These might have been used in sexual display, as a threat mechanism, or merely to keep in touch with other members of a herd.

Pentaceratops

("Five-horned face"). Forget *Pachyrhinosaurus*—this is a *real* horned dinosaur. With one spike on its nose, two long ones on its forehead, and a small one on each cheek, this ornate ceratopsian also featured an enormous neck frill. It roamed what is now the southwestern United States during the Late Cretaceous, and may have run in vast herds as the *Triceratops* did.

Pinacosaurus

("Board lizard"). There is nothing very special about this 18-foot (5.5-meter) Late Cretaceous ankylosaur. Like many of its relatives, it had bony plates protecting its skull, thick skin, and teeth designed for grinding up vegetation.

Nothing special—except it had a pair of extra holes near its nostrils. Holes that no scientist has been able to figure out the purpose of. Holes that prove once again that there is still a lot we don't know about the dinosaurs.

Plateosaurus

("Flat lizard"). Without a doubt the best-known of all prosauropods, those mysterious early relatives of the great Jurassic sauropods. *Plateosaurus* is well known for one very good reason: It was apparently very common, and many of its skeletons have survived in good condition. So we know that it reached a length of about 25 feet (7.6 meters), that it had a long but rather thick neck, and that it probably spent most of its time walking on all fours. However, it could rear up on its hind legs if it wanted to reach some succulent vegetation.

Prosaurolophus ("Before *Saurolophus*"). Sometimes it seems that scientists allow their hopes to carry them away. Hence this Late Cretaceous duckbill's name. Yes, it bore marked similarities to *Saurolophus*, which lived several million years later. Yes, it may well have been that duckbill's direct ancestor (which would make it very special, as scientists have had a terrible time tracing any sort of accurate dinosaur family tree). But, given the vagaries of the fossil record, and the sixty-five million years that have passed since the last one disappeared, who's to know for sure?

Protoavis ("First bird") Scientists have known for many years that dinosaurs and birds are closely related. Perhaps the most telling evidence of all has been the 150-million-year-old *Archaeopteryx*, that small dinosaur with a feathered tail and arms whose nineteenth-century discovery in Germany shook the scientific world. For many years, *Archaeopteryx* has been concidered the likely ancestor of modern birds.

But some scientists have long doubted that birds could have evolved directly from *Archaeopteryx*, for one good reason: such advanced birds as herons and gulls began to appear just a few million years after *Archaeopteryx's* heyday, and evolution simply doesn't work that fast.

In 1986, a Texas paleontologist named Sankar Chatterjee made a stunning announcement. He had found, he said, a fossil skeleton that contained far more bird-like qualities than did *Archaeopteryx*—but also shared many characteristics with the dinosaurs. For example, *Protoavis* (as he named it) had strong hind legs, a bony tail, and a dinosaur-like pelvis. But the skeleton also contained a bird's large eye sockets, hollow bones, a large wishbone, and a breastbone featuring a keel, used by birds to anchor flight muscles.

Perhaps most exciting of all, however, was *Protoavis'* age. It lived at the dawn of the late Triassic period, 225 million years ago. This places it seventy-five million years before the appearance of *Archaeopteryx*, and even further before the first advanced bird. Therefore, *Protoavis* may in fact be the missing link we've been seeking for decades: the world's first bird.

Protoceratops ("First horned face"). Only 6 feet (1.8 meters) long, this earliest known horned dinosaur was dwarfed by such later arrivals as *Triceratops*. It had no horns, but its curving beak, large neck frill, and other features left no doubt that it was a ceratopsian. Probably the most interesting thing about *Protoceratops* was discovered by famed explorer Roy Chapman Andrews during a 1922 expedition to Mongolia. Here Andrews came upon undisturbed nests containing eggs and skeletons of newly hatched young that he identified as *Protoceratops*. They must have died during a sandstorm or other ancient calamity.

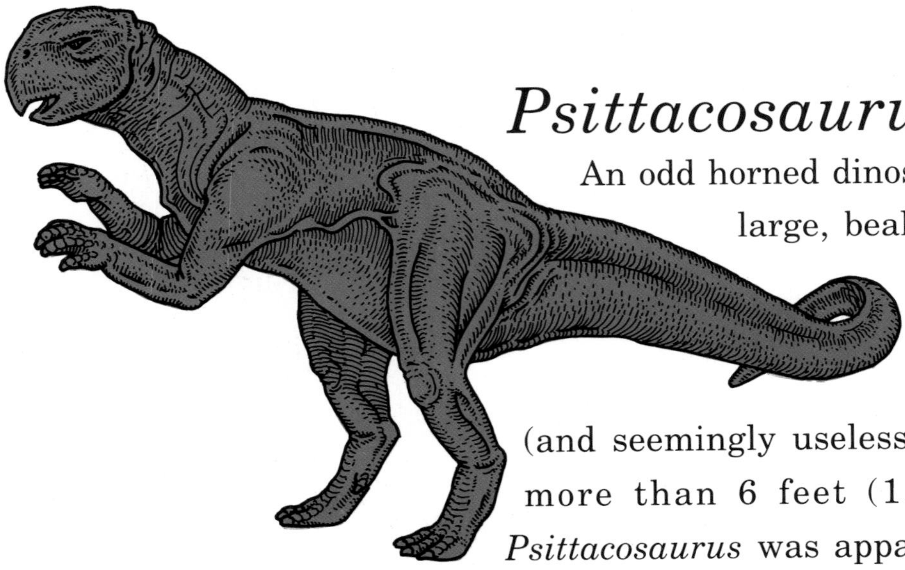

Psittacosaurus ("Parrot lizard"). An odd horned dinosaur that, aside from its large, beaked head, resembled an ornithopod more than a ceratopsian—although one type did have a tiny (and seemingly useless) horn on its nose. No more than 6 feet (1.8 meters) in length, *Psittacosaurus* was apparently comfortable both on all fours and on two legs. Its rather small front legs ended in hands that the dinosaur might have used to pull vegetation from bushes and trees.

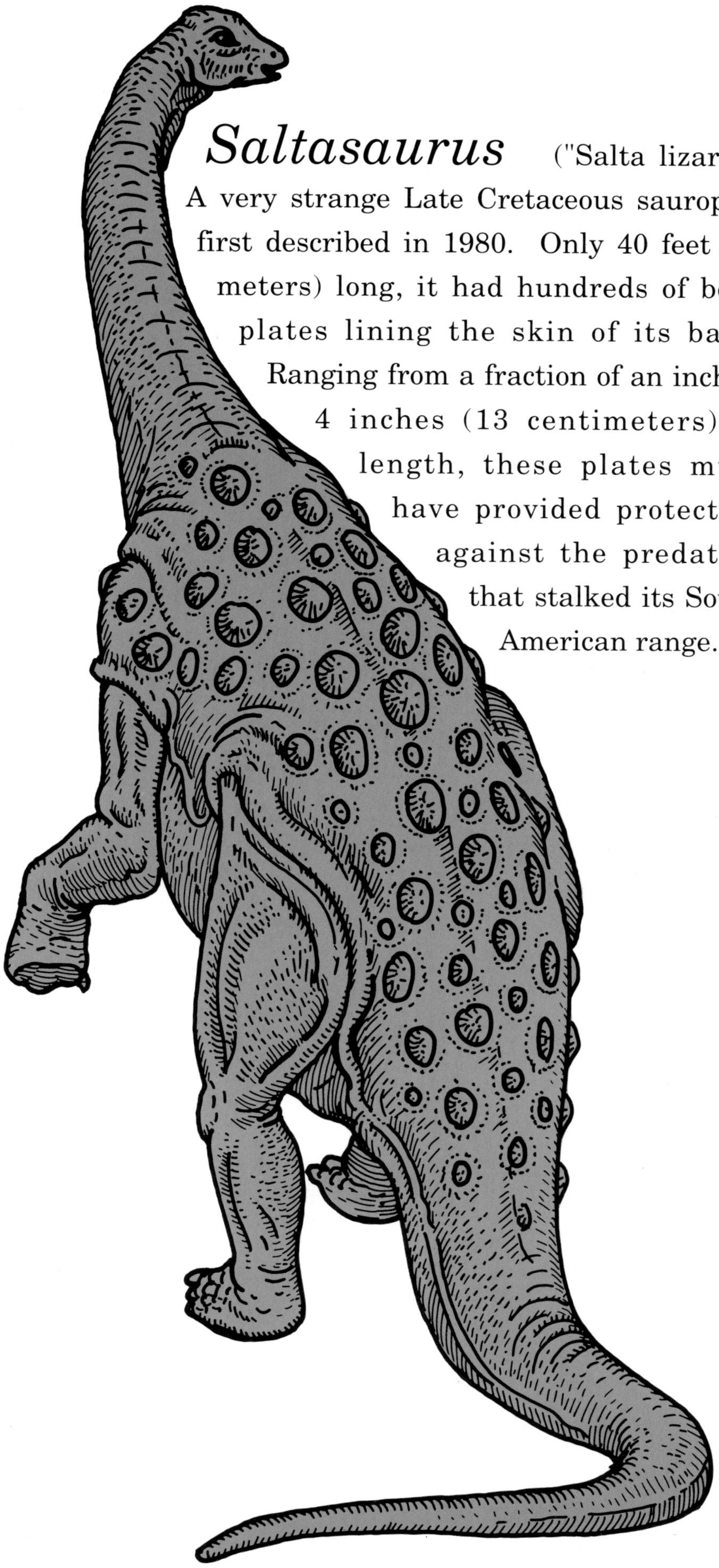

Saltasaurus ("Salta lizard").

A very strange Late Cretaceous sauropod, first described in 1980. Only 40 feet (12 meters) long, it had hundreds of bone plates lining the skin of its back. Ranging from a fraction of an inch to 4 inches (13 centimeters) in length, these plates must have provided protection against the predators that stalked its South American range.

Saurolophus

("Ridged lizard"). Every duckbill, it sometimes seems, had at least one odd characteristic. Thirty-foot (9-meter) *Saurolophus* had a strange sloping skull that scientists think was covered with flaps of skin. It may have been able to inflate these flaps into balloons, perhaps to impress members of the opposite sex.

Saurornithoides ("Birdlike lizard").

Even if most everyone loves the dinosaurs, few people think of them as having much in the way of intelligence. Yet here was a dinosaur with a brain proportionately far larger than most other reptiles'. With its huge eyes designed for accurate long-distance sighting, light frame, and sharp claws and teeth, *Saurornithoides* must have been a formidable foe. Its superb vision may have allowed it to hunt in near-darkness, when most other dinosaurs were already bedded down for the night. Some paleontologists believe that this was the same dinosaur as the *Stenonychosaurus*.

Saurornitholestes

("Lizard-bird robber"). Another in a long list of "terrible claw" dinosaurs—those remarkably intelligent and fierce Late Cretaceous descendants of *Deinonychus*. *Saurornitholestes* was far smaller, only about 6 feet (1.8 meters) in length, but it made up in weaponry what it sacrificed in size. Along with the switchblade claws found throughout the family, it boasted sharp, serrated teeth, and strong, grasping hands that ended in hook-shaped claws—perfect for grabbing and holding onto far larger prey.

Scelidosaurus

("Limb lizard"). This low-slung dinosaur, which moved slowly through Early Jurassic Europe, was one of the most primitive of all armored dinosaurs. Lacking the solid armor, large bony plates, spikes, and clubs that protected later ankylosaurs and stegosaurs, it made do with rows of small chunks of bone imbedded in its skin. Even this protection must have prevented all but the most powerful predators from attacking *Scelidosaurus*.

Scutellosaurus

("Little-shield lizard"). As *Saltasaurus* showed earlier, not only the armored dinosaurs came equipped with protection. This Early Jurassic ornithopod was only 4 feet (1.2 meters) long, so it couldn't have stood up to local meat-eaters in search of a meal. But *Scutellosaurus*, like *Scelidosaurus*, harbored hundreds of small, bony studs along its back. Presumably, a mid-sized predator might break a tooth on this thick skin, allowing *Scutellosaurus* to escape.

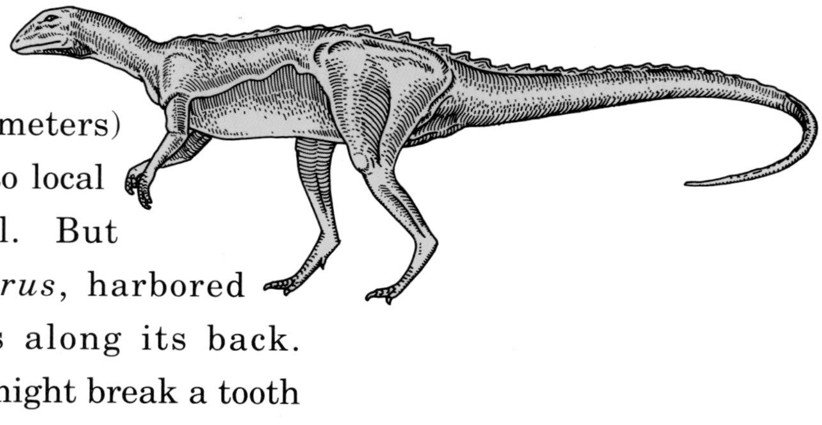

In this evocative scene, a trio of *Camarasaurs* stalk across a field of mud toward a herd of *Camptosaurs*. Unwittingly, they left behind trackways, which scientists use today to learn about how the dinosaurs lived (following page).

Segisaurus ("Segi lizard"). An odd, little-known Jurassic dinosaur that deserves mention because it doesn't seem closely related to any other dinosaur. Unfortunately (but not unusually), all that is known about it comes from some incomplete skeletons found in Arizona. From what's been studied, however, *Segisaurus* is thought to be related to the coelurosaurs, and perhaps most similar to *Procompsognathus*, with which it shares long, slender hind legs. Unlike the lightweight coelurosaurs, however, *Segisaurus* had solid bones—so it probably wasn't as agile and didn't move as fast as those fleet hunters.

Segnosaurus ("Slow lizard"). Despite more than a century of intensive searching, paleontologists still frequently come upon fossils of dinosaurs they've never seen before. Many of these, for some reason, have been found in Mongolia, a barren, harsh landscape that remains one of the richest fossil sites on earth. Beginning in the late 1970s, scientists began to uncover the remains of a group of very odd Late Cretaceous saurischians—lizard-hipped dinosaurs so unlike any others that they were soon placed in their own infraorder: segnosauria, or "slow lizards."

What made *Segnosaurus* and its relatives so unusual? First, they had many features seen previously only in bird-hipped dinosaurs. For example, *Segnosarus'* hip bones closely resembled those of ornithischians, as did its toothless beak. Yet it also had rows of sharp teeth—clearly designed for meat-eating—in the back of its jaw.

Experts think that this 30-foot (9-meter) maverick may have spent much of its time in the water, chasing and catching fish.

Seismosaurus ("Earthshaker lizard"). A little later you'll read about *Supersaurus* and *Ultrasaurus*, two enthusiastically named sauropods that—at the time of their discoveries in the 1970s—were the longest dinosaurs ever known. *Seismosaurus* comes first alphabetically, which is only appropriate, for right now this Jurassic sauropod is the biggest dinosaur ever.

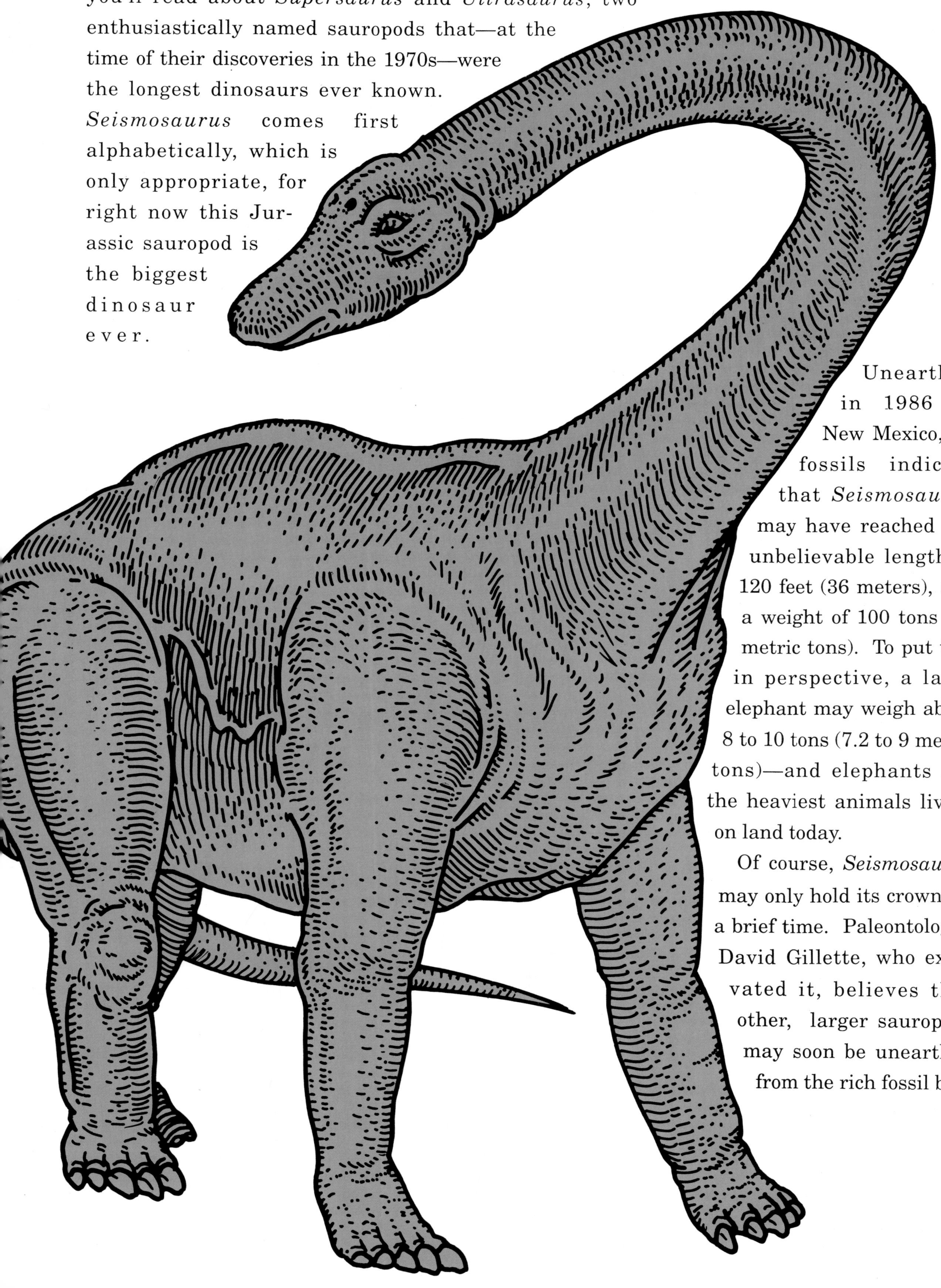

Unearthed in 1986 in New Mexico, its fossils indicate that *Seismosaurus* may have reached the unbelievable length of 120 feet (36 meters), and a weight of 100 tons (99 metric tons). To put this in perspective, a large elephant may weigh about 8 to 10 tons (7.2 to 9 metric tons)—and elephants are the heaviest animals living on land today.

Of course, *Seismosaurus* may only hold its crown for a brief time. Paleontologist David Gillette, who excavated it, believes that other, larger sauropods may soon be unearthed from the rich fossil bed.

Shantungosaurus

("Shantung lizard"). The largest duckbill yet found, this Chinese plant-eater may have been nearly 50 feet (15 meters) in length—as big as a *Tyrannosaurus*. In classic duckbill fashion, it was heavyset, with thick, strong legs and short, fleshy arms. But, unlike its more outlandish relatives, it apparently had no crest.

Spinosaurus

("Spiny lizard"). Each type of dinosaur usually boasted at least one feature that truly distinguished it from all others. Horned dinosaurs had sharp spikes and expansive neck frills; duckbills had odd, hollow crests; armored dinosaurs had impregnable skin and clublike tails. But in almost every group there is at least one (and usually many more) that doesn't fit the mold. Take a look at *Spinosaurus*, a Late Cretaceous combination of a carnosaur and a sailboat.

Forty feet (12 meters) long, with teeth like knives, *Spinosaurus* was clearly a relative of *Tyrannosaurus* and other Late Cretaceous meat-eaters. But fossil finds have proven that it had enormous spines sticking up from its backbone. These spines—some a full 6 feet (1.8 meters) long—must have supported a massive sail of skin that ran along the reptile's back. This sail, scientists believe, probably functioned as a heat exchanger, gathering the sun's rays in the cool morning and evening, allowing Spinosaurus to vent heat during the hotter parts of the day.

Staurikosaurus ("Cross lizard").

Another strange, primitive Late Triassic dinosaur, which roamed what is now Brazil. Only about 6 feet (1.8 meters) tall, lightly built, with sharp teeth, a large head, and very long tail, *Staurikosaurus* resembled both early prosauropods (which ate plants) and theropods (which ate meat). Exactly what group it fell into will not be decided until paleontologists find more fossils of either *Staurikosaurus* itself or of its close relatives.

Stegosaurus ("Plated lizard").

One of the best-known and most-beloved of all dinosaurs, this 30-foot (9-meter) armored stegosaur was also the biggest of its kind. It had a tiny head (with a brain the size of a walnut), short front legs, a huge, heavy body, and a thick, tapering tail. But *Stegosaurus*' most famous features were the large plates that ran in a row down its back, and the vicious spikes that tipped its tail.

Look in nearly any dinosaur book, and you'll see *Stegosaurus* illustrated as having *two* rows of alternating plates on its back. In 1986, however, sculptor Stephen Czerkas built a scientifically accurate model of the dinosaur showing that the *Stegosaurus*' bone and muscle structure allowed it only a single row of plates. Now most experts agree that this was the real *Stegosaurus*.

What's wrong with this picture? If you noticed that the *Stegosaurus* had two rows of plates on its back, and knew that scientists now agree that the huge dinosaur had only one row, then congratulate yourself. But do you also know what *Stegosaurus* used its row of plates for?

Like most of its duckbill relatives, *Saurolophus* had an ungainly shape, making it a comparatively awkward and slow-moving dinosaur. Though many must have fallen prey to meat-eaters, duckbills as a whole thrived during the Cretaceous.

Stenonychosaurus

("Narrow-clawed lizard"). A close relative of *Saurornithoides*, this remarkable dinosaur had an even larger brain. *Stenonychosaurus* was too small (about 6 feet [1.8 meters] in length) and too slightly built to attack larger creatures, but it probably was a very successful hunter of small mammals and lizards.

Struthiosaurus

("Ostrich lizard"). No relation to the ostrich dinosaurs, this little ankylosaur was one of the few dinosaurs you might have wanted to take home as a pet. Only 6 feet (1.8 meters) long, it may have lived only on islands (where limits of food sources would have made small size a useful adaptation). *Struthiosaurus* wore several different types of armor, including long shoulder spines, bony plates on the neck, and small spines on the sides and tail.

Styracosaurus

("Spiked lizard"). With a single long horn sticking up from its nose (and twisting horns above its eyes), this 18-foot (5.5-meter) ceratopsian more than made up for its lack of weapons with an amazing neck frill. While most horned dinosaurs had relatively unadorned frills, *Styracosaurus*' featured six long spines aimed over its back. These spines might have helped convince local predators that *Styracosaurus* was a meal not worth trying for.

Supersaurus

("Super lizard"). This is a real dinosaur, although its name will probably eventually be changed. First discovered in 1972, this sauropod was at the time the largest dinosaur ever found. It apparently spanned more than 90 feet (27 meters), and stood more than 50 feet (15 meters) high. Its neck alone was nearly 40 feet (12 meters) in length, and a single vertebra measured 5 feet (1.5 meters).

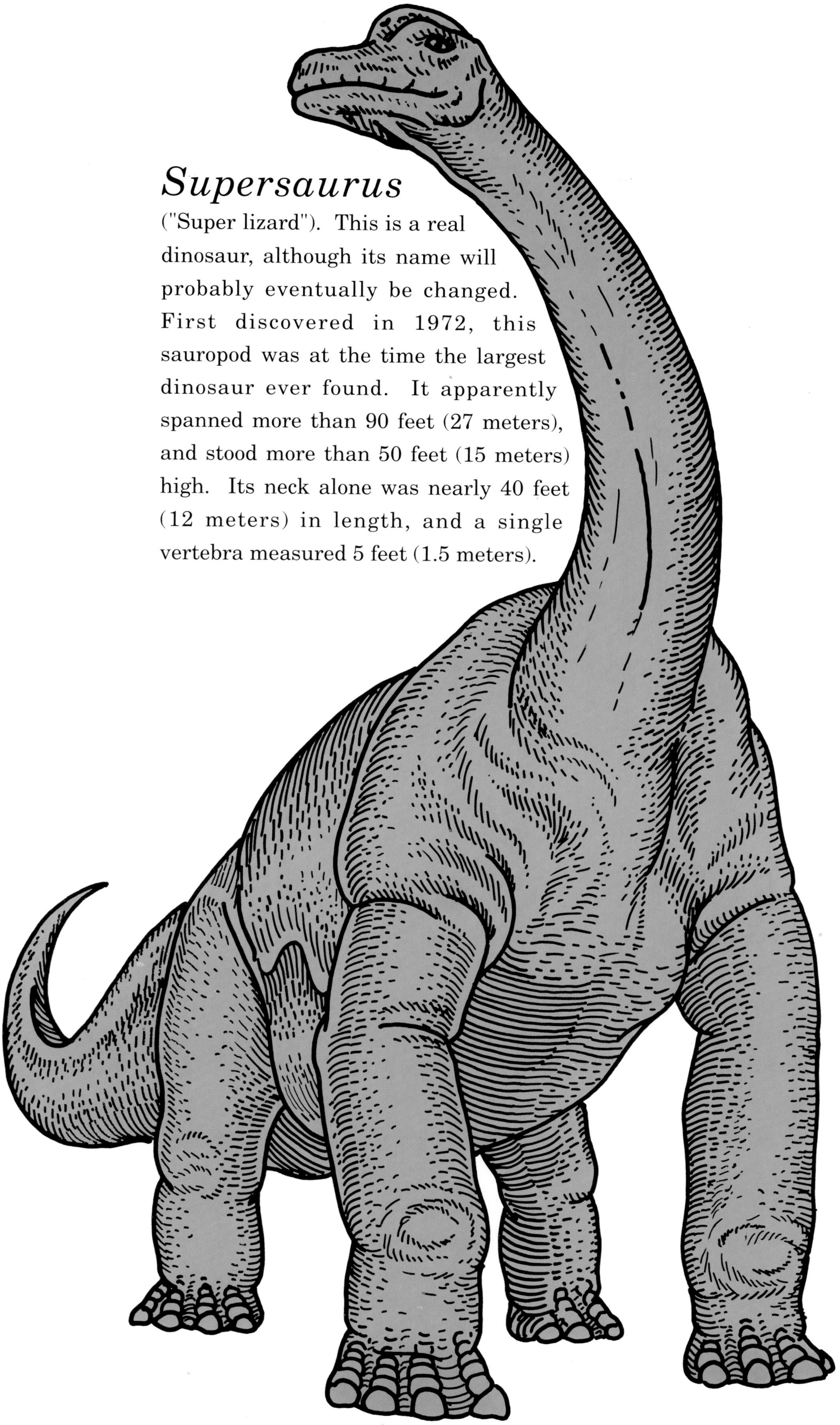

Tenontosaurus

("Sinew lizard"). A fascinatingly unusual iguanodon or hypsilophodon, *Tenontosaurus* lived in Early Cretaceous western North America. It had one of the finest tails in the dinosaur universe, a tail that took up perhaps two-thirds of its 21-foot (6.5-meter) length. It also had much longer front legs than many similar dinosaurs, leading scientists to think that it may have spent much of its time walking on all fours.

Tenontosaurus bones have frequently been found in the same fossil beds as those of *Deinonychus*, the "terrible claw." This means one of two things: either *Tenontosaurus* was a favorite prey of *Deinonychus*, or the species just shared the same habitat, and their bones ended up in the same sites.

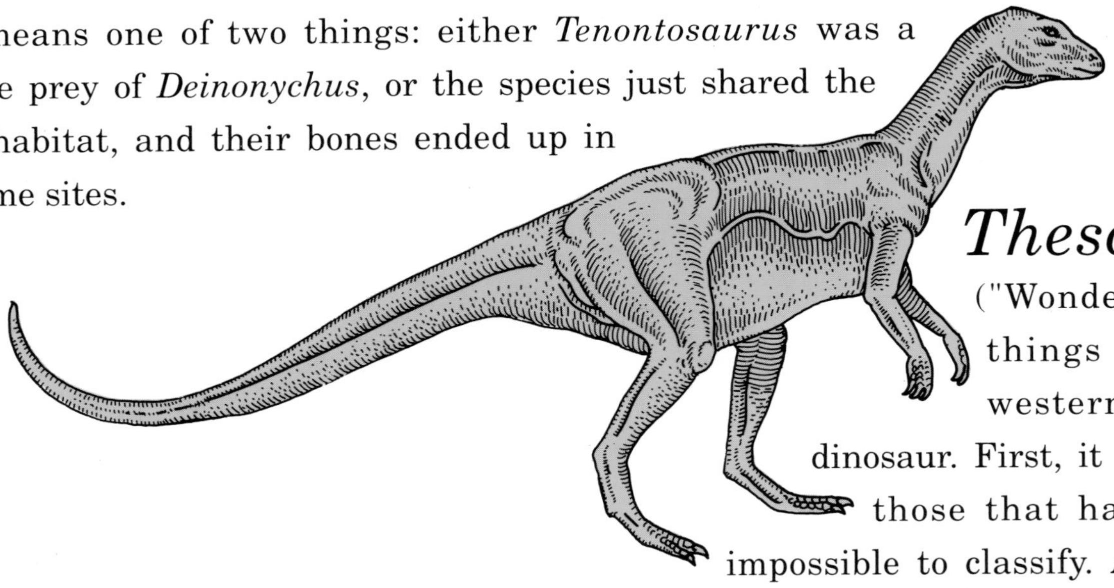

Thescelosaurus

("Wonderful lizard"). Two things distinguish this western North American dinosaur. First, it was another one of those that have proved almost impossible to classify. And second, it was one of the last dinosaurs, living at the very end of the Late Cretaceous. It died out in the great extinction sixty-five million years ago.

Thescelosaurus was a mid-sized dinosaur, reaching a length of about 11 feet (3.1 meters). It had long, slender hind legs and rather strong arms, ending in five-fingered hands. It was also one of several dinosaurs equipped with bony armor, in this case chunks of bone set into the skin along its back.

Therizinosaurus

("Scythe lizard"). Remember *Deinocheirus*, known from only a pair of 8-foot (2.5-meter) arms tipped with claws like curved butchers' knives? Well, here's another Mongolian monstrosity, a Late Cretaceous carnosaur or deinonychosaur that also had arms measuring 8 feet (2.5 meters) in length. But *this* nightmare creature's arms were far sturdier and more massive than *Deinocheirus*', and its curved claws—as strong and sharp as a scythe—may have measured a stunning 3 feet (92 centimeters) in length. Only if we're lucky enough to find the rest of *Therizinosaurus* will we know how this great meat-eater used its matchless weapons.

Triceratops

("Three-horned face"). Many groups of dinosaurs produced their largest individuals at the very end of the Late Cretaceous, right before the great extinction that doomed every last dinosaur—and the ceratopsians were no exception. There is little doubt that, at 30 feet (9 meters) in length, weighing 6 tons (5.5 metric tons), and boasting three horns that might have been 5 feet (1.5 meters) long, *Triceratops* was the most impressive of all horned dinosaurs.

Need more? Scientists now think that *Triceratops* lived and ran in huge herds. What a sight they must have made, thundering across the plains of western North America by the thousands. The whole earth would have seemed to be shaking.

Tröodon

("Wound tooth"). One of the rules of dinosaur lore is very simple: All ornithischian (bird-hipped) dinosaurs were plant-eaters. No ornithopods, boneheads, duckbills, or ankylosaurs ever touched a scrap of meat.

Enter *Tröodon*. First identified (and named) after a single, sharp, serrated tooth found in 1856, it was long thought to belong to one of the groups of meat-eating dinosaurs. Then scientists began to unearth more *Tröodon* fossils, culminating in the most complete finds yet—more teeth, jawbones, even eggs and babies discovered by John Horner and Robert Makela in 1979 and 1980.

These discoveries were remarkable, because they seemed to show that *Tröodon* was most closely related to hypsilophodons, those fast-moving dinosaurs that possessed teeth built for eating plants and plants alone. But *Tröodon*'s knifelike teeth are clearly designed for ripping flesh, so their owner may be the single exception to the grand rule: the ornithischian with a taste for meat.

Tsintaosaurus

("Tsintao lizard"). Just when you thought you'd seen all the latest styles in duckbill headgear, here comes *Tsintaosaurus*. This 33-foot (10.2-meter) Late Cretaceous dinosaur boasted a horn that stuck straight up from the top of its head like some new-wave haircut. As in *Parasaurolophus* and others, breathing tubes ran up and back within the horn, perhaps allowing *Tsintaosaurus* to produce resonant whoops and hollers.

© National Museum of Natural Science, Ottawa, Canada

Few dinosaurs were more impressive—or more abundant—than the great *Triceratops*. This massive dinosaur roamed the plains of western North America during the Late Cretaceous in huge herds, driving off predators with its sword-tipped horns.

Tyrannosaurus ("Tyrant lizard"). You've waited very patiently through dinosaurs with switchblade claws, with thick heads, with new-wave horns. Now, after dozens of less important beasts, you've finally reached the section on the most popular dinosaur of all time, the great tyrant itself. And now I'm going to have to disappoint you.

Of course, at 40 or more feet (12 or more meters) in length, *Tyrannosaurus* was one of the biggest carnosaurs of all time. And no one's arguing that it didn't have a terrifyingly massive head and 7-inch (18-centimeter) teeth that looked like meat cleavers. The only question—and it's an important one—is: What did *Tyrannosaurus* do with all this weaponry?

Today, more and more scientists think that *Tyrannosaurus* was simply too large, too massive, to be an effective hunter. Instead, they believe, it stalked around its North American habitat hunting for corpses of dinosaurs that had died of natural causes. Then it would eat. Yes, *Tyrannosaurus* may have been a Late Cretaceous carrion crow, a vulture—not a slavering merchant of death.

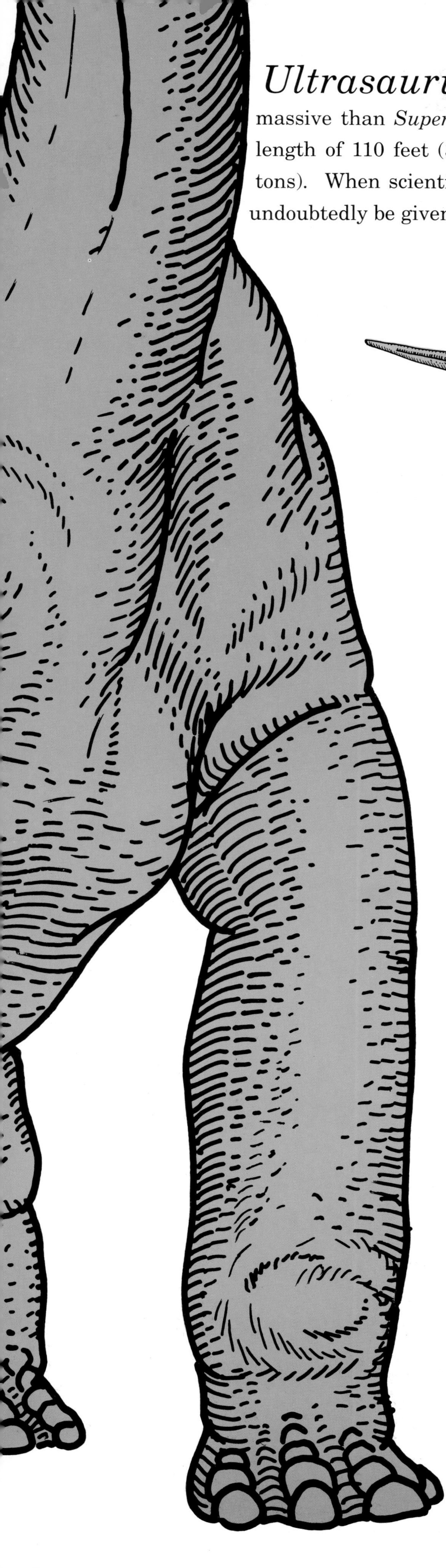

Ultrasaurus

("Ultra lizard"). Bigger than *Apatosaurus*, more massive than *Supersaurus*, this dinosaur may have reached the remarkable length of 110 feet (34 meters), and may have weighed 150 tons (131 metric tons). When scientists get around to studying and describing it fully, it will undoubtedly be given a more sober name than *Ultrasaurus*.

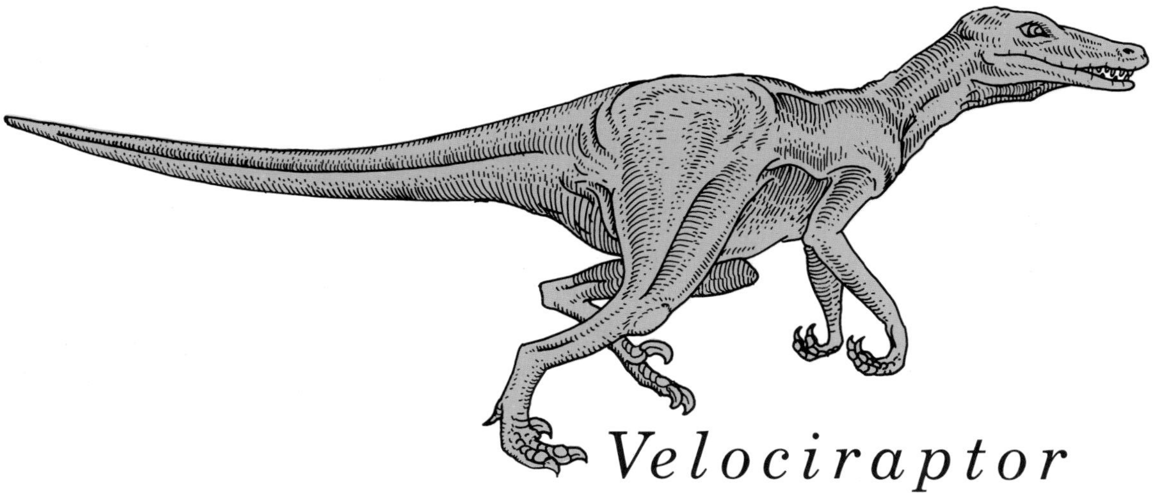

Velociraptor

("Swift robber"). Like its larger and fiercer cousin *Deinonychus*, *Velociraptor* was a quick and agile predator, equipped with sharp teeth, sharp claws on its fingers, and a large switchblade claw on each foot. Although it probably usually chased after relatively small prey, in 1971 scientists found a *Velociraptor* fossil locked in an eternal embrace with a *Protoceratops*. Apparently the hunter had attacked and disembowled the horned dinosaur. But somehow the *Protoceratops* managed to crush the *Velociraptor*'s chest at the same time, and the two dinosaurs died together.

From this *Apatosaurus* through *Velociraptor* and beyond, the dinosaurs will always capture our imaginations. **(following page)**

P A R T

3 *Digging for Dinosaurs*

Uncovering Fossils

Fossils Defined

So what exactly is a fossil, anyway?

A broad definition is easy: It's a remnant or trace of some ancient creature or plant that has been preserved in the earth's crust.

That's right, of course, but it's hardly a complete definition of what fossils are. And it completely ignores the question of how these relics of a long-gone age have managed to survive, often in remarkably intact form, for hundreds of millions of years. Yet anyone who is fascinated by dinosaurs or other extinct creatures should want to know more about fossils. For without these mementos, the dinosaurs would be truly extinct, gone forever without anyone ever knowing they existed.

In the broadest terms, a fossil is anything that has somehow remained preserved, rather that decomposing. For example, the bodies of that famous Ice Age pre-elephant, the woolly mammoth, have sometimes been unearthed from Siberian ice fields in such an intact state that they could be sliced up into mammoth steaks. Similarly, ancient insects were often trapped in amber (the hardened pitch from pine trees); today, they look as if they've been encased in tinted plastic.

But most fossils consist of only the hard parts of animals: teeth, bones, shells. Very rarely do softer objects, such as plants or dinosaur skin, become fossilized. All of these fossils are formed in a slow, painstaking way—and only when conditions are perfect. "The places where we find the most dinosaur bones aren't necessarily where the dinosaurs were most common," points out Mick Hager, director of the Museum of the Rockies in Bozeman, Montana. "Instead, at the time that the dinosaurs died, these areas were ideal for the preservation of fossils."

What makes a certain region ideal for fossils? The

Left: Abundant and widespread for many millions of years, trilobites remain among the most frequently found fossils to this day.

Below: Even the fragile wings of this ancient bee were perfectly preserved, indicating that it was quickly protected by a layer of silt after death.

Opposite page: © John Cancalosi/Tom Stack & Associates © Brian Parker/Tom Stack & Associates two most important factors are water and silt. If an ancient frog died on land, scavengers and the elements would quickly reduce its skeleton to dust. Even if it sank to the bottom of its pond, chances were that none of its remains would last; all would be consumed by scavengers or bacteria.

But, suppose a massive storm brought unusually cold weather, lowering the temperature of the pond to a level where the frog could not survive. When it died, it sank to the bottom, but before it could decompose, the fury of the storm washed a layer of silt over the body. This coat of sediment might then be covered by more, and the final blanket, many feet of hardened silt and mud, would then form a protective bed for the frog's body.

What happens to a fossil once it's been coated in this way varies. Even with the protection of the sediments, the encased creature may eventually deteriorate into nothing. What's left then is called a *mold,* an imprint in the surrounding rock that exactly mimics every detail of the long-gone animal. In the case of snails and other creatures with shells, the mold may be of either the internal or external parts of the shell.

Sometimes a shell fills with some other sediment, such as mud. When the surrounding sediment erodes, the mud breaks free. This independent imprint (always of the shell's inside) is called a *steinkern*.

Yet another possibility occurs when the hole left by a dissolved bone or shell is filled by a mineral. Then the fossil hunter will find a *cast*, a naturally formed model of a bone or shell that has decomposed. Casts are frequently composed of such minerals as calcite and pyrite.

A more subtle, gradual process occurs when a large fossil, such as a dinosaur bone, lies entombed in sediment for millions of years. Very gradually, minerals from the surrounding rock will leach into the bone, virtually replacing it. This is called *petrification*, and is perhaps best witnessed in the petrified wood of giant redwood trees in the western United States. Almost all

Below: Although nearly complete skeletons are rarely found by amateur fossil hunters, even the slightest possibility sends enthusiasts into the field.

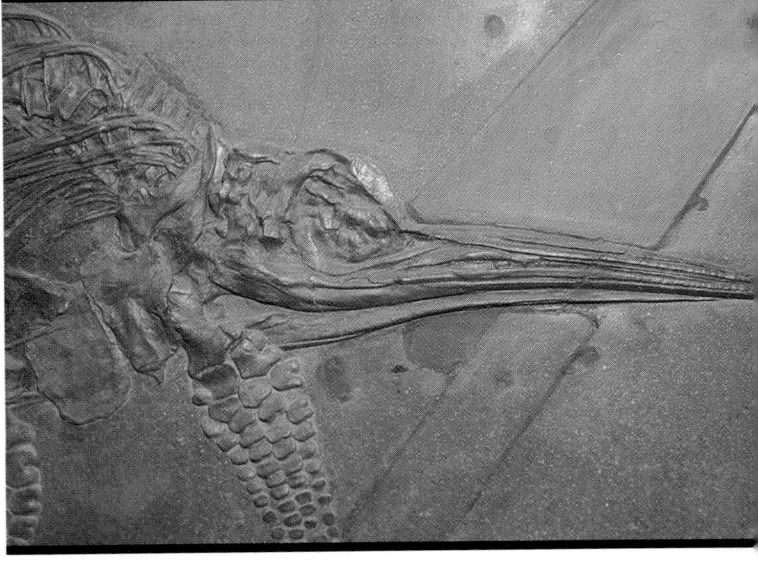

Right: Footprints, like this one left by a *Dilophosaurus* more than 150 million years ago, can tell scientists a great deal about the way dinosaurs lived.

Above: Petrified wood feels like stone, but manages to capture the delicate essence and complex details of the ancient trees that have been preserved.

dinosaur bones have undergone petrification; it's one of the processes that allows the bones to last forever.

Some of the most exciting fossils of all are not the remains of an animal, but of something it did. These *impressions* include the subtle fossilized imprint of a fallen leaf on mud, or the gentle track of an ancient snail. In recent years scientists have begun to discover large numbers of fascinating impressions: the footprints and trackways of dinosaurs.

These fossils—usually made when the dinosaurs walked through drying mud, which was then quickly covered by new sediment—have taught us that many dinosaurs traveled in herds, that some were far quicker and more agile than previously thought, and that some species may have migrated vast distances in search of food. Impressions are among the rarest of fossils. And, as is the case with many rare things, they are also among

the most valuable.

Even in areas that boasted perfect conditions for fossilization during the time of the dinosaurs, luck must be on the side of modern scientists. Countless fossils remain trapped under yards of impenetrable sediment; only those brought close to the surface by erosion or movements of the earth's crust ever become accessible. This fact makes areas like Montana and Alberta (see "Where the Dinosaurs Are", page 158)—where the fossils have ended up close to the surface—a paleontologist's dream.

Fossil quarries, like this active one, may look unprepossessing. But treasures lurk just below the surface.

Today, fossilized fish can be found anywhere from deserts to mountaintops; yet another sign of how the world has changed since ancient times.

How To Find Fossils

No matter how avid a fossil hunter you are, unless you visit the fossil beds near Pine Butte Preserve in Montana, Dinosaur National Park in Utah, or Dinosaur Provincial Park in Alberta, Canada, it is unlikely that you will find dinosaur bones. But, with the knowledge of the best places to look for fossils (and a little perseverance), you'll have a good chance to collect many fascinating remnants of ancient times.

First and most importantly, you must learn how to read the landscape. Depending upon where you live, you might be able to step outside and find a rock filled with fossil shells—but don't count on it. You are far better off knowing where to look before you begin your hunt.

Fossils occur only in sedimentary rock, the type formed when layers of silt settle and harden over the course of millions of years. Typical sedimentary rock includes limestone, shale, and sandstone—all of which are frequently home to large and small fossils.

Unfortunately, sedimentary rock is often buried deep underground. In a few areas, however, these deeply

Like ruined monuments of some ancient civilization, these fossilized giant sequoias still stand where they grew thousands of years ago.

buried layers of stone have been brought to the surface. The mountains of the northeastern United States, for example, were thrust upward by great geologic forces; in Pennsylvania and parts of New York, fossil-rich shales can be found littering hillsides. Don't expect to find dinosaur bones here, even though they do exist. Before these mountains were formed, the land lay under a shallow inland sea—so most fossils here are of early shelled sea creatures.

In other areas, water—in the form of rain and rivers—has eroded away millions of years of soil and rock, bringing a slew of fossils very close to the surface. As mentioned before, the badlands of Montana and Alberta are prime examples of erosion at work. Here, with a little training, you can find the bones of dinosaurs, flying reptiles, early mammals, and many other creatures—but it's best to go with an expert.

If you happen to visit one of these areas, pay close attention to the sides of the hills that characterize the badlands. Wherever recent wind and rainfall has washed soil down the hillside, you may find newly exposed fossils.

In most areas, however, human intervention has been necessary to uncover fossil beds. Quarries where limestone, shale, or other rock is mined for commercial use are a prime target for fossil hunters. It was in a German quarry that nineteenth century scientists found that famous dinosaur-bird, the *Archaeopteryx*. You might not find anything so exciting, but a quarry's piles of discarded scrap rock are often home to fascinating fossils. Road cuts, construction sites, and other places where large amounts of earth are moved are also promising sites for the amateur paleontologist.

Although you may be lucky enough to find a rich fossil bed on your own, you'll probably save some time by calling the closest science or natural history museum. The people there may be able to tell you about fossil-hunting trips organized by the museum, or at least recommend the best places to visit.

Though rarely as complete as this one, dinosaur trackways can be found anywhere that conditions were right during the era of the great reptiles.

Where The Dinosaurs Are

The United States and Canada are both quite rich in fossils, ranging from the vast Jurassic and Cretaceous bone beds of Alberta, Montana, and Utah to the fascinating and mysterious dinosaur trackways that crisscross much of Connecticut. Luckily, for anyone interested in dinosaurs, not all of these fossils are locked up in vaults, accessible to scientists and no one else. From one end of North America to the other, museum exhibits, parks, and preserves offer us the chance to see dinosaurs up close. Here are a few of the finest.

Modern museum exhibits follow that latest scientific evidence to produce wonderfully lifelike dinosaur models, such as this grim-faced *Allosaurus*.

"Most peculiar, Sidney... another scattering of cub scout attire."

Dinosaurs in the Wild

DINOSAUR NATIONAL MONUMENT, Utah.

This wonderful park lies in extreme northeastern Utah, a 330-square-mile (8,547-square-kilometer) stretch of western badlands containing barren gullies, eroding cliffs, and miles of desert scrub. In other words, it's a perfect place for finding dinosaurs.

First discovered during the great dinosaur hunt of the late 1870s, this fossil site became famous when scientist Earl Douglass journeyed there in 1909, under orders by steel baron Andrew Carnegie to bring back something big to fill a new wing of Pittsburgh's Carnegie Museum. Douglass soon found what Carnegie was looking for: a remarkable *Apatosaurus* skeleton taken from a rock face that was filled with countless dinosaur bones.

For more than a decade Douglass dug fossils from this hillside, finding skeletons of *Stegosaurus, Diplodocus,* and others—yet when he left, the rock face was still bursting with bones. In 1915, the area was proclaimed a national monument; more recently, a cathedral-like, glassed-in building was erected around the original quarry. Today, that atrium encloses an active fossil site 75 feet (23 meters) in height and more than 150 feet (46 meters) in length.

From the walkways along the inside of the atrium, you can watch paleontologists patiently chipping away at the rock face. Dinosaur bones are everywhere, right at the surface. You will want to climb down and dig some out yourself, but you'll have to be satisfied with a close-up look at the paleontologist's craft, along with a renewed appreciation of how many dinosaurs must have roamed these badlands—if such a small area could contain the bones of such a staggering number.

DINOSAUR PROVINCIAL PARK, Alberta, Canada.

Set along the banks of the Red Deer River, this

stretch of badlands mirrors that found a few hundred miles south, at Pine Butte Preserve in Montana. Like that site, Dinosaur Provincial Park contains some of the richest Cretaceous fossil beds in the world, dating back between sixty-four and seventy-six million years. Since early in this century, superb specimens of *Parasaurolophus*, *Corythosaurus*, and many other duckbills have turned up, along with *Albertosaurus*, *Stenonychosaurus*, and dozens of others. Many of the best skeletons can be seen virtually where they were first fossilized in the park, while others now reside in the Tyrrell Museum of Paleontology in Drumheller, Alberta.

DINOSAUR STATE PARK, Rocky Hill, Connecticut.

You've probably noticed that nearly all the most famous North American dinosaurs came from the western end of the continent. *Tyrannosaurus*, *Stegosaurus*, *Apatosaurus*, and *Triceratops* may have lived millions of years apart, but they all shared one characteristic: an affinity for the arid hill country just east of what are today the Rocky Mountains.

On the other hand, the eastern portion of the continent has yielded far fewer dinosaurs—so few, in fact, that many people think that the region simply didn't host any. But that's not true, says paleontologist Nicholas Hotton, of the Smithonian Institution's National Museum of Natural History. "If you find a layer of rock from the right era, and it doesn't contain a single fossil, then you can conclude that maybe the dinosaurs didn't live there," he explains. "But if you find even one fossil, you're probably in an area that had plenty of dinosaurs. So we know that dinosaurs did live in eastern North America, even if we don't find many fossils here."

Why is the East such a poor relation in the dinosaur game? The reason is simple: Conditions there during the Mesozoic era simply didn't encourage the transformation of bone to fossil. (See "Fossils Defined,"

Seeing is believing, but owning is even better. As well as displaying dinosaur trackways in their natural state, Dinosaur State Park in Connecticut encourages children to make—and keep—plaster casts of the huge footprints.

© Smithsonian Institution

A *Ceratosaurus* dismantles an ornithopod in this evocative Smithsonian diorama, which, like all the best dinosaur museum exhibits, provides an evocative glimpse of life during the Mesozoic.

page 151, for an explanation of how fossils are formed.) Instead, most of the dinosaurs that died simply decomposed until nothing was left. It was a rare individual that lasted long enough to be found by scientists.

None of which is to say that the dinosaurs left no signs of their lives in the northeastern United States. What they left were footprints, thousands of them. In Connecticut alone, Jurassic dinosaurs strode across vast mud fields and lake edges that then dried and hardened. The fascinating trackways that remained are now on view in Dinosaur State Park.

The park preserves more than five hundred tracks of a mysterious 185-million-year-old dinosaur whose three-toed prints remained undiscovered until 1966, when they came to light during the construction of a government building in Hartford. Visitors to the park's huge geodesic dome can follow the trackways, spot where the dinosaurs apparently began to swim, and note the variations in trackway size, indicating that this long-gone lake edge was home to young dinosaurs, as well as 20-foot (7-meter) long adults.

Interestingly, no one knows exactly who made these tracks, although they closely resemble those left by *Dilophosaurus*, an odd predatory dinosaur whose fossils have been found in Arizona. The tracks themselves were confusingly dubbed *Eubrontes*, but that's not the name of the dinosaur.

PINE BUTTE SWAMP PRESERVE, Choteau, Montana.

Paleontologists working at this Nature Conservancy preserve along the eastern front of the Rockies don't have to settle for dinosaur trackways. Instead, they can pick from a host of fascinating fossils of dinosaurs and other Cretaceous creatures, including *Maiasaura*, *Albertosaurus*, *Orodromeus*, *Tröodon*, pterosaurs, and early mammals. As an added attraction, nearly all of

© Chad Slattery

Perhaps the most dramatic exhibit of fossils in the world is preserved at Utah's Dinosaur National Monument, where expert guides lead tours of a hill filled with dinosaur bones.

these fossils lie amazingly close to the surface of the ground; many can be spotted actually eroding out of the earth.

For the amateur dinosaur enthusiast, Pine Butte isn't as easy to reach as the above parks—but it's worth the effort. Only at Alberta's Dinosaur Provincial Park can you achieve the same pure sense of walking where the dinosaurs once ruled, and nowhere else can you dig up a *Maiasaura* shinbone, collect fragments of dinosaur eggshell, or—if you're lucky—find a shiny, black dinosaur tooth lying on the ground, as if its owner had just dropped it there. (For an in-depth profile of Pine Butte Preserve and its dinosaur marvels, as well as details on how to participate in a dig there, see "Pine Butte: Dinosaur Mecca" on page 167.)

Dinosaurs in Captivity

Q: *What's the most important reason that so many of us are entranced by the dinosaurs?*

A: *Museums.*

With their great echoing halls, their burnished skeletons, their dioramas of life in the Mesozoic era with

Not only dinosaurs show up in dinosaur halls. This pristine mammoth, looking very much like a modern elephant, dominates its exhibit at the National Museum of Natural History.

© Smithsonian Institution

© Smithsonian Institution

Nowhere else can you get as close to actual dinosaurs than at science and natural history museums, which often boast carefully reconstructed skeletons like this one.

painted backdrops so real that you feel you could step right into them, museum exhibits are the best opportunity most people have of getting close to the dinosaurs. And North America's wealth of fascinating permanent displays, ranging from old favorites to futuristic new exhibits, don't disappoint.

AMERICAN MUSEUM OF NATURAL HISTORY, New York City, New York.

This superb museum contains what may be the most famous dinosaur hall in the world. It certainly has the most extensive collection on the planet, including such priceless specimens as the "mummified" *Anatosaurus*, a hulking *Apatosaurus*, a nearly complete *Tyrannosaurus* that has given generations of children nightmares, *Protoceratops'* eggs, and a remarkable variety of horned and ornithopod dinosaurs.

CARNEGIE MUSEUM OF NATURAL HISTORY, Pittsburgh, Pennsylvania.

Andrew Carnegie was one of the richest men in the world at the end of the nineteenth century, and leaving a legacy in his museum was one of his prime goals. As a result, Carnegie's dinosaur hall has a wonderful collection, especially of such Jurassic titans as *Allosaurus*, *Apatosaurus*, and *Diplodocus*.

FIELD MUSEUM OF NATURAL HISTORY, Chicago, Illinois.

Like the National and American Museums, the Field Museum is one of North America's most venerable museums. Among the most satisfying of its many dinosaur skeletons is its *Albertosaurus* in the act of consuming a *Lambeosaurus*.

MUSEUM OF THE ROCKIES, Bozeman, Montana.

Now safely ensconced in new, larger quarters, this museum can boast some of the most in-depth and innovative dinosaur displays ever unveiled. Paleontologist Jack Horner works out of here; not surprisingly, the museum concentrates on the spectacular recent finds that he and his associates have been making in the Montana badlands. With dioramas, stunning paintings, and—of course—a wealth of specimens, the museum carefully delineates the fascinating life of *Maiasaura* and many other dinosaurs found in the same area.

© Chad Slattery

How big were the dinosaurs? At the Dinosaur Valley Museum in Grand Junction, Colorado, you can get up-close-and-personal with a *Brachiosaurus* arm bone and find out for yourself.

NATIONAL MUSEUM OF NATURAL HISTORY, Smithsonian Institution, Washington, DC.

The Smithsonian Institution's dinosaur hall is far smaller than its neighbor in New York. But when the renovated exhibit opened in 1981, it was clear that its designers had worked hard to create an informative tour through the age of the dinosaurs. Dioramas, films, and skeletons of *Albertosaurus*, *Diplodocus*, and many others all contribute to the hall's haunting mood.

PEABODY MUSEUM OF NATURAL HISTORY, Yale University, New Haven, Connecticut.

If you want to see where some of the spoils of the Bone Wars (see "Dinosaur Hunters," page 173) ended up, here's where to look. Many of Othniel Charles Marsh's nineteenth century finds ended up here, including such treasures as *Allosaurus*, *Camptosaurus*, and *Othnielia*, a tiny Jurassic ornithopod named after Marsh in 1977.

Of course, this is a woefully incomplete listing. Many other museums—in the United States, Canada, and worldwide—boast important dinosaur collections. And it seems as if new exhibits are appearing every week. Check your local museums to see what they're offering.

ROYAL ONTARIO MUSEUM, Toronto, Ontario, Canada.

This enormous museum contains an extensive gallery of dinosaur exhibits. All concentrate on North American specimens, including such Canadian treasures as *Albertosaurus*, the odd duckbill *Lambeosaurus*, and the ostrich dinosaur, *Ornithomimus*.

TYRRELL MUSEUM OF PALEONTOLOGY, Drumheller, Alberta, Canada.

A center for some of the most important research into dinosaur behavior, located amid the glories of Alberta's overwhelmingly rich Cretaceous fossil beds, this museum now displays many of the most important dinosaurs found in the region. Their particular emphasis is on the duckbills, many of which were unearthed within the borders of Dinosaur Provincial Park.

Even in real life, there is something creepy about a hall filled with dinosaur bones.

The beautiful Pine Butte Swamp Preserve, whose forests, fens, and badlands harbor grizzly bears, bighorn sheep, whooping cranes—and a slew of dinosaurs.

Dinosaur Mecca
Pine Butte

There is a place of magical, barren beauty along the eastern front of Montana's Rocky Mountains. Gaze east, and the Great Plains, punctuated by mushroomlike buttes, stretch to the horizon under a stunningly big sky. Turn westward, and the mountains rise with stark abruptness, their peaks seeming newly carved by the whistling, ever-present wind.

Here, grizzly bears descend from their mountain haunts and stalk across the prairie, searching for the tubers and berries that make up so much of their diet. Bighorns clash in the constant struggle for domination of the herd. Whooping cranes—perhaps the world's rarest birds—stop by on their migratory journey toward the Canadian wilderness.

But the Nature Conservancy's Pine Butte Swamp Preserve is home to more than North America's rarest and most exciting wildlife. Eighty million years ago, countless thousands of dinosaurs died here in a vast volcanic ashfall. Together, wind and water have combined to weather away millions of years of sediment—so if you visit the preserve with an expert guide, you'll soon see the perfect fossil remains of more dinosaurs than you imagined possible. You'll also be haunted by the presence of the great reptiles in a vivid, overwhelmingly immediate way that museums, movies, and books simply cannot provide. On the badlands of Pine Butte, every time you look over your shoulder you expect to see a dinosaur stroll by.

Pine Butte Swamp Preserve and the adjoining areas protect perhaps the most important fossil site ever found. For it was here that paleontologists Jack Horner and the late Robert Makela first came upon the nests, eggs, and young of *Maiasaura*, the "good mother lizard" whose breeding habits have revolutionized our view of the dinosaurs (see "Dinosaur Behavior," page 57, and "Dinosaurs A to Z," page 83, for details). This patch of rugged prairie is also home to the remains of horned dinosaurs, hypsilophodonts, weird carnivorous dinosaurs, early mammals, and dozens of other fascinating creatures.

But what makes Pine Butte so special is that you can get down on your knees and actually participate in a search for the dinosaurs. Both the Nature Conservancy and the Museum of the Rockies in Bozeman, Montana, operate one-day to one-week digs centered at the area's richest site: Campasaur Quarry. "Campasaur is one of the only places on earth where you can bring people, give them instructions in digging, and then guarantee that they'll find bones," says paleontologist Mick Hager, director of the Museum of the Rockies.

© S. AvRutick

Hardy pine trees manage to survive, but, luckily for scientists, the erosion of the earth is inexorable throughout the preserve.

Campasaur has had an amusing history. Horner and others were digging at a distant site, but had chosen to camp here, on a comparatively flat area, not far from the road. One day, a member of the team attempted to pitch a tent, and found that his tent stakes wouldn't penetrate the earth. When he searched for the obstruction, he found *Maiasaura* bones, lots of them. Thus, the Campasaur Quarry was born.

The paleontologists then dug a few test pits, and found an unbelievably rich lode of fossils, as many as thirty bones per square meter of soil. "We were able to see that this geologic horizon—the layer of sediment set down at the time that these dinosaurs died—stretched for about three miles by one-quarter mile (five kilometers by .4 kilometers)," Horner recalls. "We think that, at a conservative estimate, ten thousand *Maiasaura* must have died here in the ashfall that followed a volcanic eruption."

For the visitor, this wealth of fossils means the chance to play paleontologist, if only for a day. First, the resident scientists lead visitors to the site (a rather unimpressive stretch of broken ground only a few yards long) and explain what to look for. Then everyone is given a tiny pick (really more of a large awl) and a brush, and the digging begins.

Within a few minutes, a yell indicates the first find: the dark edge of a large bone protruding from the earth. With great care, its discoverer brushes away the loose soil, picks away a clutter of rocks, and gradually unearths a 2-foot (60-centimeter) long *Maiasaura* leg bone. It looks as if it were buried last year, not eighty million years ago. And it lies in its shallow bed alongside dozens of other remains of these 30-foot (9-meter) dinosaurs, ranging from jaws to toe bones.

As new bones are uncovered, the amateur paleontologists swab them with a quick-hardening glue to protect the fragile fossils from disintegrating. Next, the exposed portions of the bones are swathed in plaster, which is then left to dry. Finally, the bones are carefully lifted from their age-old site, to be taken to the Museum of the Rockies, where Horner and others will continue their studies of *Maiasaura* life. "This is the most delicate part of the operation," says Mick Hager. "Every paleontologist has carefully unearthed and prepared an

Though much of Pine Butte's prairie can seem gentle and unthreatening, thousands of years of harsh weather have helped bring the fossils of *Maiasaura* and other dinosaurs to the surface.

important fossil, doing everything right, then reached to lift it and seen the bone fall out of the plaster in a heap."

The opportunity to get your hands dirty among *Maiasaura* bones isn't the only experience awaiting those on a visit to the Montana badlands. As a meandering hike quickly shows, the area is full of signs of an ancient, dinosaur-filled world—although trying to understand it without an expert nearby is as impossible as translating a foreign language without a dictionary.

With someone to explain it, however, you see that every layer of rock, every dry, crumbly gully, adds a piece to the dinosaurs' story. For example, one subtle pattern indicates the presence of an anastomosing river (one that never overflowed its banks), whose edges served as the *Maiasauras*' exclusive choice for nesting sites. The crumbly soil underfoot? You're standing in an ancient lake bed that feels as if it just drained yesterday.

And fossils are everywhere, eroding out of the earth with each day of biting winds or sudden storms. The bank of a dry river may reveal the backbone of a dinosaur sitting like tiny steps leading down to the streambed. Nearby, on the slope of a small hill, are specks of flat, black stone: pieces of *Maiasaura* eggshell, indicating the presence of a nest above. Elsewhere, close inpection of hunks of reddish or blackish stone reveal the odd textures and hidden channels of fossil bone. A lucky visitor may even stumble upon the perfectly preserved tooth of an *Albertosaurus*, a Cretaceous carnosaur. Shining in the sunlight, its sharp edges gleaming, the tooth looks new—and again the visitor may feel as if its owner is about to come striding around the nearest hill.

Pen ready, the author watches an amateur paleontologist in action. At Pine Butte's Campasaur Quarry, a shovel, a small broom, and a pick are the only necessities for finding dinosaur bones.

Campasaur Quarry is not the only site open to those traveling to Pine Butte. Nearby lies Egg Mountain, an eroding knoll that in ancient times was an island in a shallow lake. Egg Mountain was first discovered in 1979, when Jack Horner looked at a flag left by a seismic crew—and saw an intact dinosaur egg sitting at its base. "Luck plays a large part in many discoveries, but only if you're in the right place to be lucky," Horner says. "That was the first intact egg ever found in the Western Hemisphere."

Further digging at Egg Mountain uncovered a remarkable number and variety of fossils. Horner and his team soon found many more eggs, which they identified as belonging to an 8-foot (2.4-meter) long hypsilophodont whose bones are found in numbers nearby. (The dinosaur now goes by the name *Orodromeus makelai.*) Other fossils included smaller eggs that Horner thinks belonged to *Tröodon,* a predator that probably ate the hypsilophodont eggs and babies; small mammals that may have scavenged around the nest sites; and the remains of a pterosaur with a 30-foot (9-meter) wingspan, lying virtually undisturbed in the lake bed.

Visitors to Egg Mountain get the chance to see many of these fossils—and maybe even discover some new ones of their own. "It's remarkable how often someone who's never searched for fossils will come here, and almost immediately make an important find," says Mick Hager. "Everyone who visits these sites has a real chance of contributing greatly to our knowledge of Cretaceous dinosaurs."

To find out more about visiting Pine Butte Swamp Preserve and participating in a dinosaur dig, contact the Nature Conservancy in Arlington, VA; the Pine Butte Guest Ranch in Choteau, Montana; or the Museum of the Rockies, in Bozeman, Montana.

A prized find near Campasaur Quarry, this pristine *Albertosaurus* tooth will help scientists at the Museum of the Rockies learn more about the Cretaceous carnosaur.

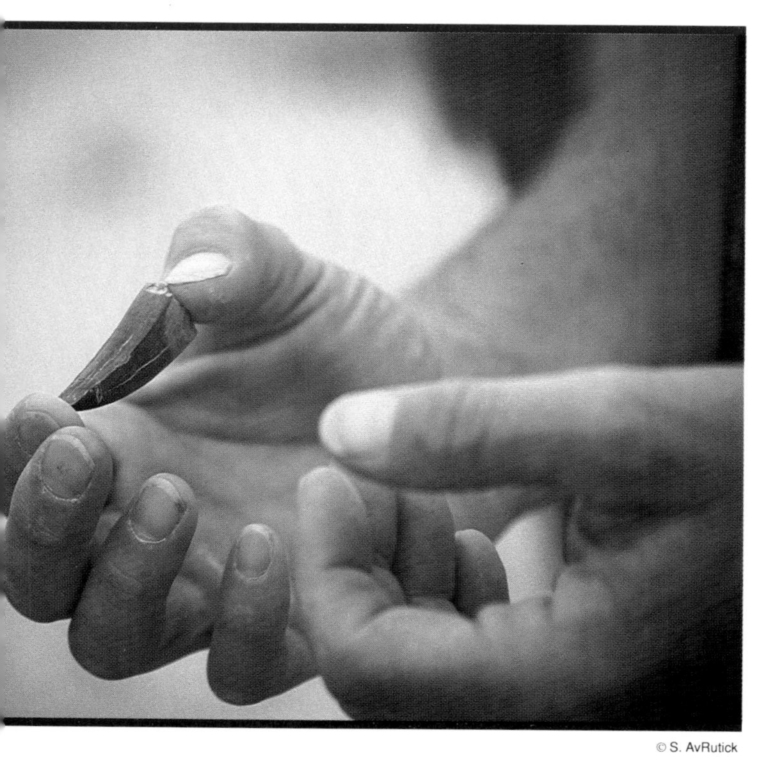

© S. AvRutick

The spirit of adventure. Looking more like gunslingers than paleontologists, this Yale College crew prepared to head west to search for fossils in 1872. (Charles Marsh is in the middle of the top row.)

Dinosaur Hunters

The history of dinosaur hunting is filled with eccentrics, odd people who risked their lives (not to mention their reputations) to journey to the harshest, most remote regions on earth. Even today, a fair share of paleontologists are people who would much rather camp out in barren badlands than face a class of interested students. Maybe there's something about the hunt for the ancient fossils of long-dead creatures that attracts loners.

Surprisingly, the legend that surrounds the first discovery of a dinosaur bone (or at least the first whose discoverers knew they'd found something unusual) is one of the nicest in all of dinosaur-hunting history. This, of course, is the tale of Dr. Gideon Mantell, his wife, Mary Ann, and a road near their home in Sussex, England.

One day in 1822, the story goes, Mary Ann Mantell was out for a walk when she spotted something odd sticking out of a pile of earth beside the road. Close inspection revealed that it was a huge tooth, surrounded by others. She quickly called Gideon (an avid fossil hunter), who confirmed her suspicions. Mary Ann had made a truly sensational find: the remains of some giant, ancient lizard whose existence had never before been suspected.

This is a nice story, with all the right elements of surprise, luck, and success. Unfortunately, both Gideon Mantell's own papers and other contemporary reports leave Mary Ann out of the picture entirely. It was Gideon who found the tooth, people say now, not Mary Ann.

Whatever really happened, there's no question that Gideon Mantell was farsighted enough to identify the tooth as belonging to a huge, plant-eating reptile that lived during the Cretaceous. He named it *Iguanodon*, because its teeth resembled those of a modern (though much smaller) lizard, the iguana.

The moment all paleontologists dream of: making a discovery that you know will revolutionize the field.

"What a find, Williams! The fossilized footprint of a brachiosaurus! . . . And a Homo habilus thrown in to boot!"

The Mantells's discovery was followed by many others, most spectacularly those of the British geologist William Buckland. He'd actually discovered odd bones and teeth in an Oxford quarry in 1818, but didn't report his conclusions about them until 1824. These were clearly the fossils of another Cretaceous reptile, he said, but one very different from the *Iguanodon*. It had long, sharp teeth that left no doubt that it was a meat-eater. *Megalosaurus* was the name Buckland gave to this great reptile, a name it still holds today.

Although these and other discoveries ignited a fossil-hunting craze in England, it wasn't until the 1841 meeting of the British Association for the Advancement of Science that someone took the next great imaginative leap forward. The man was Richard Owen, a brilliant and famously obnoxious paleontologist who proposed the existence of a group of huge reptiles, the dinosaurs or "terrible lizards" that had once populated England and—he thought—the rest of the world, too. Their fossils merely awaited discovery.

Following this stunning announcement, scientists and amateurs alike began searching for dinosaurs in Europe, the United States, and elsewhere. None, however, were as successful—or as eccentric—as Othniel Charles Marsh (1831-1899) and Edward Drinker Cope (1840-1897). As famous during the height of their careers as any baseball superstar is today, these two men captured the imagination of the American and European public—in part because they kept making astounding fossil finds, and in part because they simply could not abide each other.

Even before they began reporting their remarkable discoveries, the two scientists feuded fiercely. Though they had begun with a wary mutual respect (even naming early fossil finds for each other), their relationship soon soured. Apparently, the uncrowded world of nineteenth century paleontology was too small for them, and by 1870 their once friendly correspondence had degenerated into name-calling.

Braving fiery temperatures and using primitive tools, modern paleontologists (like these at Wyoming's Fossil Butte National Monument) use the same painstaking methods as their forerunners did a century ago.

Edward Drinker Cope's pugnacity, intelligence, and bitterness are all apparent in this early portrait.

Among the famous dinosaurs first discovered by Othniel Charles Marsh were *Allosaurus*, *Stegosaurus*, and *Triceratops*.

The ultimate rift, however, didn't occur until 1872. That was the year Cope virtually snuck into one of Marsh's prime digging sites, an area in Wyoming and adjacent Utah that contained interesting early mammal fossils. Hiring a guide previously employed by Marsh, Cope dug up some bones, spirited them back home, and quickly published descriptions of his finds.

If he had spent years planning the action that would most infuriate his rival, Cope could not have made a better choice. For the rest of their lives, the two men despised each other to distraction—yet their hatred both brought dinosaur hunting into the public eye and led to many of the greatest North American fossil discoveries ever made.

The sites of Cope and Marsh's Bone Wars (as the feud came to be known) were the vast, dinosaur-rich lands lying east of the Rocky Mountains, but Como Bluff, Wyoming was the special prize. This remarkable badlands region (just a few miles in length) held the bones of vast numbers of previously unknown Jurassic dinosaurs, including some of the most famous dinosaurs of all. Between 1877 and 1889, each scientist fought to be the first to dig up and take home the fossils that would cement his place in history (and, just as important, ruin his rival).

Cope and Marsh did their jobs well. Marsh's team was the first to uncover *Apatosaurus*, *Stegosaurus* (at the time the first plated dinosaur ever found anywhere), the great carnosaur *Allosaurus*, and dozens of others. Cope, struggling with more limited resources, still managed to unearth the thick-necked sauropod *Camarasaurus*, the fascinating predatory *Coelophysis*, and many others.

How important were these two warriors to the history of paleontology? Before they entered the picture, dinosaur hunters found only nine dinosaur species in all of North America. Between them, Cope and Marsh added 136 species to the list. And scientists are still sifting through the tons of bones that the two shipped to museums from Como Bluff and other sites. They have one major problem: Because Cope and Marsh's teams were sworn to secrecy, and the two men obviously never spoke, they tended to discover the same dinosaurs, yet give them entirely different names. It was up to later scientists to untangle the classification mess.

The Bone Wars lasted far beyond the height of Cope's and Marsh's success. To his death, Cope remained convinced that he had been cheated of true recognition by his rival, and was forced to watch bitterly as honor after honor was bestowed upon Marsh. It would certainly infuriate both of these brilliant scientists that even today, their names are always mentioned in the same breath.

For some reason, after Cope and Marsh, dinosaur hunters lost some of their seductive eccentricity (or maybe they just weren't observed as closely). Throughout the late nineteenth and early twentieth centuries, paleontologists like Joseph B. Tyrrell, Barnum Brown, and Charles H. Sternberg added greatly to our knowledge of North American dinosaurs. In the western United States and Canada, they unearthed the bones of countless duckbills, carnosaurs, and others—but without ever provoking a new rivalry to match that of Cope and Marsh.

This century has seen fossil hunters study in the ancient rock of every continent on earth. A team of German paleontologists, led by Werner Janensch, braved the wilds of Tanzania in 1907 to bring back remains of *Brachiosaurus* and hundreds of others. Fifteen years later, the American Museum of Natural History sent Roy Chapman Andrews to the perilous Gobi Desert of Mongolia, where he discovered a slew of new dinosaurs, including *Oviraptor* and *Protoceratops*. In recent years, teams of paleontologists have found increasing numbers of dinosaur bones in Australia, South America—even Antarctica.

Today's paleontological community is populated by many brilliant and strong-willed scientists—and they

Marsh's fossil-filled classroom at Yale. Note the early comparison of birds and dinosaurs on the lower right.

At Pine Butte's Campasaur Quarry, scientists follow the methods of earlier times by erecting tepees, which withstand the biting winds far better than modern tents do.

have a lot to argue over. Were dinosaurs warm-blooded? What was their social life like? How did they die? Skirmishes over these and other issues erupt at every scientific meeting, and even a cursory survey of the field will uncover quiet battles and public squabbles.

Still, there will probably never be another Bone War. As nearly any paleontologist will tell you: They would gladly trade in the cult of personality that fed the egos of early fossil hunters for the endlessly fascinating discoveries that characterize modern paleontology.

Every paleontologist hopes to make a find to equal Roy Chapman Andrews' great discovery in the Mongolian desert: A nest of Protoceratops eggs.

Courtesy RKO General Pictures

No one said they had to be realistic. Godzilla (here apparently zapping a man dressed up as King Kong) was just one in a long line of movie dinosaurs that terrified willing audiences throughout the world.

Dinosaurs At The Movies

Every year we see more and more dinosaur paraphernalia flood the marketplace: dinosaur stamps, dinosaur earrings, dinosaur plush toys. The great reptiles, it seems, have become the salesman's dream, the guaranteed best-seller. Most of these items will, without a doubt, be forgotten minutes after their arrival—only to be replaced by others. Anyone for dinosaur muffin tins?

But one medium's love affair with the dinosaurs has shown remarkable longevity. For more than seventy years, dinosaurs have been appearing on the silver screen, gracing both big-budget classics and mangy Z movies. And, even if they never get their names in the credits, movie dinosaurs have managed to give every dinosaur enthusiast some vivid memories. Not to mention more than a few nightmares.

The Last Frontier

The first known appearance of a dinosaur in a motion picture took place in 1915, when early special-effects expert Willis O'Brien unveiled *The Dinosaur and the Missing Link*, a five-minute movie featuring clay dinosaurs animated using the stop-motion technique. In this method (still in use today), only one frame is shot at a time, with the clay figures moved a tiny bit between frames. When run at normal speed, the resulting film seems to show dinosaurs walking, albeit a bit creakily and unevenly.

In 1919, O'Brien used the same method in *The Ghost of Slumber Mountain*. This more ambitious effort ran about fifteen minutes, and combined animation with live actors in a story about a remote, hidden valley that harbored *Allosaurus*, *Triceratops*, and other dinosaurs. Of course, the movie said, such a valley was a dream.

Still, *The Ghost of Slumber Mountain* staked out

territory that would remain a central focus of dinosaur movies for years to come. This was the idea of the Last Frontier, the distant, untracked region that still held dark and dangerous—but intoxicating—secrets. At a time of such revolutionary developments as the telephone and the airplane, the world was already beginning to seem small. Movies, as they always have, could provide an element of wildness, of danger, missing from everyday life. From the start, dinosaurs were an integral part of that exciting fantasy world.

The appeal of the Last Frontier was never as clearly stated as in the *The Lost World*, another O'Brien opus. Based on Arthur Conan Doyle's famous novel, this 1925

Scientifically inaccurate but artistically stunning, one segment of Disney's *Fantasia* featured *Stegosaurus*, *Tyrannosaurus*, and other dinosaurs to the stirring sound of Stravinsky's "Rite of Spring."

feature told the story of an intrepid team of explorers who journey to an isolated, flat-topped mountain in Venezuela. There, they find a caveman and an assortment of dinosaurs, including a *Brontosaurus, (Apatosaurus),* which they attempt to bring back to London. Of course, it escapes and destroys much of the city—the first (but certainly not the last) time that a

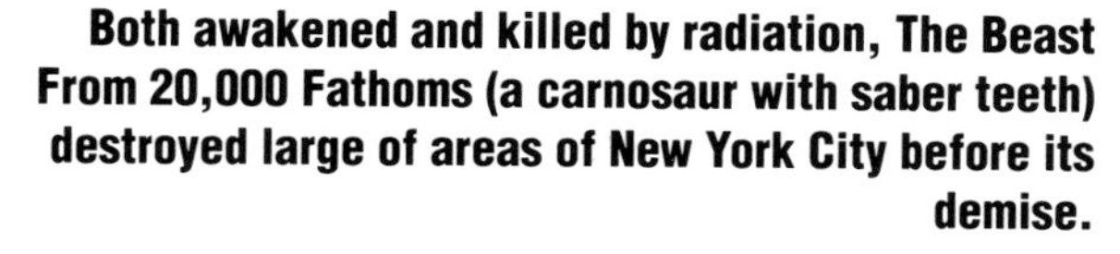

Both awakened and killed by radiation, The Beast From 20,000 Fathoms (a carnosaur with saber teeth) destroyed large of areas of New York City before its demise.

Courtesy Warner Communications

dinosaur would lay waste to a nation's capital, and a sobering reminder of how even the new metropolises could not contain the forces of nature.

Willis O'Brien achieved his first great success with the remarkable animation sequences in *The Lost World*, but his greatest work lay eight years ahead. Only in 1933, after the advent of sound had revolutionized the film industry, did O'Brien reach the pinnacle of his career. That year, he handled the special effects for another movie about a remote wilderness, a destroyed city, and a rampaging beast. But this time the beast was an ape, the city New York, and the film *King Kong*.

In this classic the dinosaurs take a back seat to Kong himself—but they're there. Remember? The great

A sauropod suffering from a seeming case of rigor mortis, Disney's *Baby: The Secret of the Lost Legend* marked a dismal return of the dinosaur to the big screen in 1985.

reptiles populate the island where Kong rules, wreaking havoc with the brave crew of adventurers and causing Fay Wray to let loose with some satisfying screams.

For some reason, the dinosaur movie disappeared soon after the phenomenal success of *King Kong*. The public's taste in horror ran more toward vampires, werewolves, and other monsters, while fantasy movies dwelled on space exploration (as in the Flash Gordon serials) or cute lions, scarecrows, and tinmen.

There were a couple of exceptions. Dinosaurs thundered across a tumultuous earth in a segment of Walt Disney's *Fantasia* (1940). And, Cary Grant did play a bumbling paleontologist to Katherine Hepburn's dizzy heiress in 1937's *Bringing Up Baby*.

Still, more than two decades would pass before the great reptiles would make more than a half-hearted further appearance. And when they did, it would be in a far darker, more frightening guise.

"There are some things Man is not meant to know..."

The 1950s were host to a remarkable outburst of science fiction and horror movies. The post-war boom, the promise of space flight, the technological revolution—all contributed to the slew of speculative films that lit up movie screens for the entire decade.

But two overriding developments dominated the themes of nearly every 1950s fantasy, from the lowest-budget programmer to Hollywood blockbusters. The developments? Communism and the atom bomb, of course. A terrifying fear existed that the world had changed beyond all imagining; that no matter where we lived, we could all die in our beds, at any time, without warning, from the twin killers of a communist attack and radiation.

Some 1950's movies, like *On the Beach*, dealt with nuclear holocaust head-on. But most approached the two subjects from the side, telling cautionary tales couched in the language of science fiction. In *Them*, nuclear tests resulted in a plague of gigantic ants. *Invasion of the Body Snatchers* told of aliens who looked just like us, but felt no emotions, and aimed to take over the world; its original ending had the protagonist staring out at the audience, saying, "You're next!" *The Thing* had a similar ending: a man shouting over a radio, "Watch the skies!"

Dinosaur movies may have reached their lowest ebb with 1975's *The Land That Time Forgot.*

In other words, paranoia ran deep—and what better image to frighten an already nervous populace than the familiar dinosaur? Dinosaurs with death and destruction on their minds, creatures that we couldn't avoid, even if we left the wilderness behind and lived in the biggest cities.

A perfect example was *The Beast from 20,000 Fathoms*, a 1953 release in which a huge dinosaur is awakened by a nuclear explosion in the Arctic. It immediately sets off for New York, bearing a cargo of deadly germs (read radiation) and looking for its age-old breeding grounds. It arrives, tramples its share of people and buildings, and is eventually dispatched by a radioactive harpoon.

As well as serving as the usual cautionary tale about the atom bomb, *The Beast from 20,000 Fathoms* introduced special-effects master Ray Harryhausen, a former student of Willis O'Brien's, who would be as influential in 1950s and 1960s science fiction films as his mentor was two decades earlier. Like O'Brien, Harryhausen used stop-motion to conjure up dinosaurs, giant insects, and other monsters.

There were other dinosaurs in 1950s movies, but none more famous or influential—or more clearly a metaphor for the atomic bomb—than a certain Japanese *Tyrannosaurus*. Making his first appearance in 1954, Godzilla used his radioactive breath to destroy vast portions of Japan, including Tokyo and other cities. Later he turned to defending the country from ever-more-ridiculous monsters (Mothra, Megalon, the Smog Monster), but at first the giant dinosaur seemed to serve as a terrifying catharsis for people who had survived the real bomb less than a decade earlier.

The New Generation

Eventually, the aura of post-war paranoia dwindled away, and with it the rash of science fiction movies that brightened the otherwise dull movie screens of the 1950s. Dinosaurs didn't disappear again (as they had in the 1940s); they just weren't potent metaphors, and the movies that contained them weren't very interesting.

One Million Years B.C. (1966) was a good example. It boasts enjoyable effects by Ray Harryhausen (never mind the anachronism of dinosaurs living alongside cavemen a scant million years ago). But if you remember this movie at all, you remember it for one thing: the sight of Raquel Welch and her cohorts in skimpy animal skins. Admit it—that's what you recall most clearly.

Ray Harryhausen was still active in the 1960s, but most of his films dealt with Jason, Sinbad, and other figures from mythology and featured flying harpies and jousting skeletons. He did venture back into dinosaur territory with 1969's *The Valley of the Gwangi*, a tired variation on the old Last Frontier motif, with cowboys in Mexico finding a dinosaur-filled valley. But no one went to see it, just as no one went to see the woeful *The Land That Time Forgot* (1975), which didn't even have stop-motion effects, only models on wires.

The 1980s have been even more barren. Disney's *Baby: The Secret of the Lost Legend* (1985) starred a young sauropod that was far more lifeless than anything Willis O'Brien ever created. And, though *Caveman* (1982) had cute special effects (including a dinosaur with adorably long eyelashes), it also featured Ringo Starr and too many dumb jokes.

But things have finally begun to look up. In 1988, gifted animator Don Bluth (a long-time associate of Steven Spielberg), unveiled the feature-length cartoon *The Land Before Time*, about the quest of a bunch of adorable baby dinosaurs. Maybe, if we're lucky, a new trend has just begun.

The dinosaurs in *King Kong* and other movies spurred the artist Doug Henderson's life-long fascination with the great reptiles, as shown by this endearing childhood painting. Today, Henderson's haunting images (seen throughout this book) are capturing a new generation of children.

Dinosaur Paraphernalia

© Chad Slattery

© Chad Slattery

© Chad Slattery

How can we not love the dinosaurs? They've been gone for sixty-five million years, but they still show up everywhere from television shows to toy stores and gas stations.

© Chad Slattery

Bibliography

Bakker, Robert T., *The Dinosaur Heresies: Unlocking the Mystery of the Dinosaurs and Their Extinction*. New York: William Morrow, 1986.

Benton, Michael, *The Dinosaur Encyclopedia*. New York: Simon and Schuster, 1984.

Brosnan, John, *Future Tense: The Cinema of Science Fiction*. New York: St. Martin's, 1978.

Charig, Alan, *A New Look at the Dinosaurs*. New York: Facts on File, 1983.

Dixon, Dougal, *The New Dinosaurs*. Salem, Massachusetts: Salem House, 1988.

Dixon, Dougal, Cox, Barry, R.J.G. Savage and Brian Gardiner, *Dinosaurs and Prehistoric Animals*. New York: Macmillan Publishing Company, 1988.

Gross, Renie, *Dinosaur Country*. Saskatoon, Saskatchewan: Western Producer Prairie Books, 1985.

Horner, John R. and Gorman, James, *Digging Dinosaurs*. New York: Workman Publishing Company, 1988.

Lambert, David, *A Field Guide to Dinosaurs*. New York: Avon, 1983.

______________, *A Field Guide to Prehistoric Life*. New York: Facts on File, 1985.

McLoughlin, John C., *Archosauria: A New Look at the Old Dinosaur*. New York: Viking, 1979.

Paul, Gregory S., *Predatory Dinosaurs of the World*. New York: Simon and Schuster, 1988.

Thompson, Ida, *The Audubon Society Field Guide to North American Fossils*. New York: Alfred A. Knopf, 1982.

Wilford, John Noble, *The Riddle of the Dinosaur*. New York: Alfred A. Knopf, 1985.

Index

ADDITIONAL CREDIT INFORMATION

Part 2, Dinosaurs A to Z: Line drawings by Robert Frank/Melissa Turk & The Artist Network.

Pages 11 and 36: © Doug Henderson/from *Dawn of the Dinosaurs*, by Robert A. Long & Rose Houk, published by the Petrified Forest Museum Association.

Page 37: © Doug Henderson/Albuquerque Museum of Natural History.

Pages 8-9, 44, 56, and 73: © Doug Henderson/Collection of the Museum of the Rockies.

Pages 10-11, 18-19, 45, 55, 60-61, 62, 67, and 68: Paintings by Eleanor M. Kish. Reproduced with permission of the National Museum of Natural Sciences, Ottawa, Canada.

Pages 78, 79, 80, 157, and 177: Courtesy Department of Library Services, American Museum of Natural History.

Pages 43, 52, and 54: Courtesy Tyrrell Museum of Paleontology, Ottawa, Canada

THE FAR SIDE cartoons are reprinted by permission of Chronicle Features, San Francisco, California.